CONSIDER MY SERVANT JOB

CONSIDER MY SERVANT JOB

An Interpretive Guide for Preachers and Teachers

A. WENDELL BOWES

THE FOUNDRY
PUBLISHING

Copyright © 2021 by A. Wendell Bowes

The Foundry Publishing®
PO Box 419527
Kansas City, MO 64141
thefoundrypublishing.com

ISBN 978-0-8341-4000-4

All rights reserved. No part of this publication may be reproduced, stored in a retrieval system, or transmitted in any form or by any means—for example, electronic, photocopy, recording—without the prior written permission of the publisher. The only exception is brief quotations in printed reviews.

Cover design: **Rob Monacelli**
Interior design: **Sharon Page**

Unless otherwise indicated, all Scripture quotations are from the Holy Bible, New International Version® (NIV®). Copyright © 1973, 1978, 1984, 2011 by Biblica, Inc.™ Used by permission of Zondervan. All rights reserved worldwide. www.zondervan.com. The "NIV" and "New International Version" are trademarks registered in the United States Patent and Trademark Office by Biblica, Inc.™

The following version of Scripture is in the public domain:

The King James Version (KJV)

The following copyrighted versions of Scripture are used by permission:

The Common English Bible (CEB). © Copyright 2011 Common English Bible. All rights reserved.

Good News Translation® (Today's English Version, Second Edition) (GNT). Copyright © 1992 American Bible Society. All rights reserved.

The Message (MSG), copyright © 1993, 2002, 2018 by Eugene H. Peterson. Used by permission of NavPress. All rights reserved. Represented by Tyndale House Publishers, Inc.

The New American Standard Bible® (NASB®), copyright © 1960, 1962, 1963, 1968, 1971, 1972, 1973, 1975, 1977, 1995 by The Lockman Foundation. www.Lockman.org.

The New Revised Standard Version Bible (NRSV), copyright © 1989 National Council of the Churches of Christ in the United States of America. All rights reserved.

Library of Congress Cataloging-in-Publication Data
Names: Bowes, A. Wendell, author.
Title: Consider my servant Job : an interpretive guide for preachers and teachers / A. Wendell Bowes.
Description: Kansas City, MO : The Foundry Publishing, [2021] | Includes bibliographical references. | Summary: "This book is an interpretive guide of the book of Job, to assist those who want to teach and preach its lessons"— Provided by publisher.
Identifiers: LCCN 2021003721 (print) | LCCN 2021003722 (ebook) | ISBN 9780834140004 | ISBN 9780834140011 (ebook)
Subjects: LCSH: Bible. Job—Commentaries. | Bible. Job—Study and teaching.
Classification: LCC BS1415.53 .B688 2021 (print) | LCC BS1415.53 (ebook) | DDC 223/.107—dc23
LC record available at https://lccn.loc.gov/2021003721
LC ebook record available at https://lccn.loc.gov/2021003722

The internet addresses, email addresses, and phone numbers in this book are accurate at the time of publication. They are provided as a resource. The Foundry Publishing® does not endorse them or vouch for their content or permanence.

To
all the ministerial students who attended my classes,
may you find this book helpful in your preaching ministry
and may it encourage you to spend more time in the Old Testament.

And with many thanks to
the faithful Nazarenes in Port Elizabeth, New Jersey;
Bristol, Pennsylvania; and Selinsgrove, Pennsylvania,
who listened expectantly to my sermons
and taught me so much about preaching.

And especially to
John,
our family's preacher in the making.

CONTENTS

Preface — 9
Abbreviations — 11
Introduction — 13
   Preliminary Considerations — 14
   Introductory Sermon — 18

I. Job 1–2: Prologue — 23
   Supersaint — 23
   Reasons for Serving God — 27
   When Life Goes Topsy-Turvy — 31
   "The Lord Gave . . . the Lord Has Taken Away" — 35
   Friends — 38

II. Job 3: Job's Anguish — 43
   Dealing with Bitterness — 43
   Life's Pathway — 50

III. Job 4–27: The Three Friends — 53
   Eliphaz — 55
   Bildad — 66
   Zophar — 75

IV. Job 4–27: Job's Responses to His Friends — 83
   Job's Condition — 83
   Three Brief Glimpses of Hope — 88
   Taking God to Court — 93
   A Violent God — 98

V. Summary of the Dialogues — 103
   Three Blind Mice — 103

VI. Job 28: Interlude — 107
   The Way to Wisdom — 107

VII. Job 29–31: Job's Manifesto   113
    Before the Calamities, I Was Living a Fantastic Life   113
    After the Calamities, I Wanted to Die   114
    I Do Not Deserve All This Suffering   118

VIII. Job 32–37: Elihu   121
    A Young Whippersnapper Takes on Job and His Friends   121
    God as Creator   124
    God as Sovereign   125
    God as Just   126
    God as Free and Mysterious   128
    God as Communicator   130
    God as Disciplinarian   133

IX. Job 38–41: God's Speeches   135
    An Awesome God   135
    God's System of Justice   138
    God's World   141

X. Job 40:3-5; 42:1-6: Job's Response to God   145
    Only a Novice Trying to Correct an Expert   145
    Who Am I?   149

XI. Job 42:7-17: Epilogue   153
    And He Lived Happily Ever After   153

Conclusion   157
    Major Theological Themes   157
    The Purpose of the Book of Job   162
    Trust in God   165

Appendix: Biblical Illiteracy   169

References   173

PREFACE

When I finished my research for my commentary on Job, I realized I had a lot of practical material left over that was more relevant to preaching and teaching than it was to a commentary. I also discovered that there are very few books on preaching from Job. So I began a second book on Job that focused on insights for preaching and teaching.

Many books on preaching are simply a collection of sermons that have been edited into book form. Such is not the case with this book. So far, I have used few of these ideas in the pulpit, although I may in the future. I am primarily interested in identifying and elucidating the main topics that preachers and teachers might find useful in creating a series of sermons or lessons on Job.

I am indebted to Ben Boeckel, Heidi Bowes, Jerry Hull, George Lyons, and Ralph and Lynn Neil for reading early drafts of this manuscript and making comments from their areas of expertise. I am also appreciative of my wife, Ginger, for her skill in proofreading. But I owe the greatest debt to my heavenly Father for his encouragement and guidance.

Job is an incredible book written by an ancient literary genius. I hope my writing efforts will encourage more usage of this book in ministry and more preaching and teaching from the Old Testament in general.

ABBREVIATIONS

General

→	see another part of the book at
AD	anno Domini (precedes date)
ANE	ancient Near East
BC	before Christ (follows date)
cf.	compare
ch(s).	chapter(s)
ed(s).	editor(s); edition
e.g.	*exempli gratia*, for example
etc.	*et cetera*, and the rest
HB	Hebrew Bible
i.e.	*id est*, in other words, that is
no(s).	number(s)
NT	New Testament
OT	Old Testament
trans.	translated by
v(v).	verse(s)
vol(s).	volume(s)

Modern English Bible Translations

AT	author's translation
CEB	Common English Bible
GNT	Good News Translation (Today's English Version)
KJV	King James Version
MSG	The Message
NASB	New American Standard Bible
NIV	New International Version (2011 ed.)
NRSV	New Revised Standard Version

INTRODUCTION

Preaching from the OT is a lost art in many American churches (→ Appendix: Biblical Illiteracy). Few sermons are based on OT texts, and those that are, are sometimes guilty of misinterpretation. One of the rationales I hear from preachers is, "No one ever showed me how to do it."

It may be true that there are few good role models for us to emulate, but that should not deter today's ministers from using the 78 percent of the Bible that we call the OT. There are rich preaching resources here if we will make the effort to use them. I hope this book, along with my earlier commentary on Job, will help to rectify this situation. Job is simply too important a book to leave out of a preacher's sermon schedule.

Effective OT sermons require input from three sources:

First, ideally, ministerial training should include courses in all the books of the Bible, since the Bible is the primary source for all our preaching. But colleges and seminaries cannot require this, because it would considerably lengthen the time of ministerial preparation. Instead, they require a general introduction to the Bible and a few in-depth studies of individual books or groups of books. The assumption is that once students have learned good principles of exegesis and interpretation in a few books, they can then apply those principles to all the books of the Bible. This means that ministers must become lifelong learners to be effective in preaching from Genesis to Revelation. And to be a lifelong learner, preachers need good scholarly resources in their personal libraries.

So scholars have an important role in preaching. They need to produce commentaries and other written tools that elucidate the basic content of all the biblical books, providing themes, topics, and possible ways of looking at the text. And preachers need to invest in these scholarly resources to help them preach effectively through the entire Bible.

Second, preachers also have an important role to play. Our part is to select the material that is appropriate, organize it, create a captivating introduction and conclusion, provide good illustrations and humor where needed, and make application to a specific congregation. A catchy title and a passionate delivery also add to the effectiveness of a sermon. In addition, our part requires us to prepare our hearts through prayer, listening to what God wants to say through us on any given Sunday. The truth of God's Word needs to impact our own lives before we present it to our congregations.

The third part of the three-legged stool is God's part. He is needed to bless what we have labored over, using it to enlighten, to encourage, to invite, to convict, to save, and to make holy those who listen. We cannot force him to honor our preparation, but usually he does. And sometimes he even blesses our preaching despite inadequate preparation.

If each of us do our part, then God has promised "through the foolishness of our proclamation, to save those who believe" (1 Cor. 1:21, NRSV).

Preliminary Considerations

1. Invest in Some Good Commentaries

One of my seminary professors encouraged my classmates and me to preach through the Bible a book at a time in the first years after seminary. And to do that effectively, he urged us to purchase at least a half-dozen good commentaries to use in the research on each biblical book. If a new pastor would do this consistently over a ten-year period, he or she would preach well Sunday by Sunday as well as eventually create an excellent, solid library for the remaining years of ministry. Some of the commentaries on Job that I have found helpful in recent years are Balentine, Clines (3 vols.), Gordis, Hartley, Newsom, and Seow. There are many others as well, but these are especially thorough (see my bibliography in my commentary [Bowes 2018] for additional resources).

2. Make Use of Several Different Versions That Employ Different Theories of Translation

Ideally, preachers should work from the Hebrew text, but this is not possible for most. Few have had a course in Biblical Hebrew, and even those who have will struggle with the text of Job, for it has many

Introduction

grammatical difficulties (see "Introduction: Text" in Bowes 2018, 33). So most preachers will have to rely on some good English translations. Use some of the best, for a sermon can never be better than the translation on which it is based.

Prior to the Reformation, there was only one translation of the Bible approved for Christian usage—the Latin Vulgate. But the influence of the Reformation has produced an abundance of good translations today. The church is truly blessed with this turn of events.

Because translators must make a choice of words when rendering a Hebrew sentence into English, there are inevitable interpretive decisions and biases that appear in every translation. Wise preachers will avail themselves of several different translations in order to arrive at a correct interpretation of a text. The issue is not to identify which translation is good and which is bad, for each has strengths that can contribute to the overall understanding. Rather, the goal should be to seek out the translation that best conveys in English the original meaning of the passage in its context. At a minimum, you should use at least one translation of a more literal style (e.g., NASB, NRSV), at least one of a rather free style (e.g., GNT, MSG), and at least one somewhere in between (e.g., CEB, NIV).

Every translation is guided by a set of principles, usually established beforehand by the publisher of the translation. "Literal" means the translators were interested in conveying a word-for-word equivalency, as much as possible. This usually results in a fairly accurate text, but the style is sometimes stilted and awkward. "Free" signifies a translation that tries to convey the thoughts of the biblical writer without overdue concern for the actual Hebrew words. Some are basically just paraphrases. These translations are usually easy to read, but they present major problems for those who are trying to find the equivalent Hebrew word. The third style, what Fee and Stuart call "functional equivalence" (2014, 44), draws from both of the above approaches and combines them into a form that is dynamically equivalent but not bound by the rigidness or freedom of the other styles. Sometimes it succeeds in this endeavor, and other times it does not. For a deeper explanation of these translation styles, see Fee and Stuart (2014, ch. 2).

As for choosing which translation to read from the pulpit, you may first want to discover your congregation's preferences. You may find that people today are bringing a wide variety of versions to church. You will have to choose one to use on a regular basis, but there is nothing wrong with pointing out better renderings of specific verses in other translations.

3. Give Yourself Adequate Time for Preparation

Job is a difficult book to exegete and interpret. It demands a preacher's best skills in sermon preparation. There are almost as many interpretations of it as there are interpreters. Consequently, you need to spend adequate time in thoughtful meditation, reading from a variety of authors and viewpoints before ever attempting to preach from it. Because there are a few places in the book where no one knows the correct translation or interpretation, a humble attitude is needed in approaching this book that has challenged preachers in every generation. But I have no doubt that every preacher can do it. Just allow sufficient time for reflection and study.

4. The Book Is Literature, but for Preaching and Teaching, Treat It as a Historical Story

I suggested in my commentary that there may have been a real character named Job who experienced much suffering and then found relief (Bowes 2018, 35-36). But we have very little evidence to prove that. So it is best not to get into the issue of historicity in the pulpit. This is a scholarly issue that has little preaching value. Most parishioners are more interested in how the book applies to them.

It might be informative to the congregation to note the literary format of the book in an introductory sermon. The beginning and ending of the book are narrated in a prose format that suggests a familiarity with an earlier, perhaps oral, story about a man named Job. But then, in between, the author created a poetic masterpiece using a massive vocabulary and a multitude of literary forms for the interaction between Job and his friends. This suggests that the author was a very creative and intellectual writer whom God used to fashion this book.

The literary character of the book should not hinder you in telling the story as if every last detail of the book were factual. Jesus utilized the same method of preaching in his use of parables, such as those of the good Samaritan and the prodigal son. In fact, the literary character of the book opens up many opportunities for preachers who are gifted in storytelling. Everyone likes stories, so take full advantage of this characteristic.

5. Tell the Story

Many people have heard of Job's name and make an immediate association with the topic of suffering, but few know all the details of his life, the different views of his friends, the meaning of God's speeches, or the conclusion that restores his relationship with God. So it is imperative that you *tell the story* when preaching from the book of Job. This has the further advantage of maintaining a high interest level in the progress of the story. A book that has a story line ties the congregation into the entire series from beginning to end. People begin to see interconnections throughout the book and start anticipating where the story will go next.

Short summaries of previous sermons at the beginning of a message help to keep the entire congregation up to date on the progress in the story. And at the end of a message, hints at topics that will be covered in future sermons create an atmosphere of expectation that will encourage congregants to read ahead in the book and return the next Sunday. A sermon series in this format will keep your entire congregation in tune with the book. And it will be appreciated by those who have to miss a sermon somewhere in the middle of the series.

6. Take Advantage of the Timeless Nature of the Book

Everyone experiences unjust suffering, and everyone would like an explanation of its cause. The questions raised by suffering are common to all humanity. So the topics in the book of Job are just as relevant today as they were in the days of the author. There is a timelessness about this book that encourages people to investigate its meaning and its application to them. In Job preachers have a ready-made topic of interest that can be used to get people thinking about their relationship with God and their possible reaction if intense suffering should ever impact their own lives.

7. Plan to Preach a Series of Sermons on Job over Several Months

Job is a long book with many characters and points of view. There is simply too much to cover in one sermon. The book requires a series of sermons that delves into its major themes and evaluates the viewpoints of the major characters. Preachers need to help congregations grapple with some of the questions raised by the book, and this takes time. That means putting aside the lectionary for a few months and focusing on this book alone. If done well, your congregation will appreciate your efforts to teach as well as preach from this little-used book.

John Calvin preached 159 sermons from the book of Job (20 are reprinted in English translation in Calvin 2011). While that feat has probably never been repeated by anyone else, it does illustrate that there is a great deal of theologically important material in this book that needs to be preached. My book attempts to help preachers do this by providing over three dozen potential sermon topics. Some are well developed. Others are mainly concepts that need further expansion. Not all need to be used. Choose what seems appropriate for your congregation at this particular time in the life of your church. A solid series of sermons from this great biblical book will enlighten and inspire any congregation over several months. May God bless each of you in this endeavor!

8. A Word to Teachers

While this book is primarily directed at preachers, I believe that teachers will also find it useful in Sunday school classes and Bible study groups. The format in these settings allows for a deeper and lengthier study of a biblical book than is possible in a typical worship service. In addition, the informality of a Bible study allows for meaningful interaction between teacher and students on some of the great theological issues and questions that the book of Job raises. This is a major advantage that teaching has over preaching. My hat is off to all teachers who would tackle a book like Job and seek to convey its meaning to their students. May your efforts be rewarded again and again with new insights and a greater appreciation for this outstanding book!

Introductory Sermon

Any series of sermons needs a good introductory sermon to establish a solid background for what will follow. This sermon should (1) provide some basic information about the book, (2) clear up misconceptions people have gathered from rumor and secondhand sources, (3) lay out the general direction where the sermons are headed, and (4) invite the congregation to journey along with the pastor in the weeks ahead. If brave, you might even ask congregation members to submit email questions they would like addressed during the course of the series.

Introduction

Here are some of the points that need to be mentioned in an introductory sermon on Job. Others can be gleaned from the introductions to commentaries on Job.

- The book tells the life story of a man who experienced horrendous tragedy and suffering. We have no way of proving whether all the events in the book actually happened as described or whether this is only literature, but there is a possibility that a man named Job actually lived at some point in the distant past. If so, his homeland was probably Edom or northwestern Arabia (today, the area of southern Jordan or northwestern Saudi Arabia).
- The setting for the book is the patriarchal period (no temple, priesthood, sacrificial system, or king), but many internal factors suggest that the actual writing occurred much later (middle of the first millennium BC or later) by a very skilled, but unknown author (see my "Introduction: Date" in Bowes 2018, 29-33).
- The author used a non-Hebrew setting for his book and non-Hebrew characters to help readers of all cultures wrestle with some of the great human questions of all time without getting bogged down in nationalistic, Israelite concerns. This reveals something of his genius as a skilled writer and creative thinker.
- The story of one man's suffering and his search for answers is the framework that the author chose to guide the action and dialogues, but underneath the surface are some significant concepts about God and the cosmos and our place in the cosmos. These theological topics will be explored throughout this series of sermons.
- Innocent human suffering is a topic that has perplexed humanity since the beginning of time. Many other books from the ancient world discussed this topic centuries before the author of Job. The biblical author may have borrowed some of his ideas from these earlier works, but he is the only one who approached this topic from a monotheistic viewpoint. Such a viewpoint creates additional problems for understanding suffering that earlier books did not have to face. For example, if only one God exists, he must be responsible for causing/allowing unjust suffering. Why would he want to do this?
- The book of Job is one of the books in the Bible known as the Wisdom Literature. The other books are Proverbs, Ecclesiastes, and Song of Songs. As a whole, the Wisdom Literature presents

Introduction

itself as a careful observer of human life. It claims to have examined and recorded both animal and human behavior over centuries of time, thus arriving at a universal understanding of life that is true and proven. But Job begs to differ. His claim is that his life does not fit the typical mold of human experience.
- The book is a literary gold mine. It begins with a prose prologue that introduces us to the main characters and ends with a prose epilogue that resolves the book's tensions and sends Job off into the sunset living happily ever after. In between, the author creates an extensive poetic masterpiece of literature centered around a series of speeches between Job and three friends who come to comfort him.

Once the basic facts of the book have been presented, the next step is to build a bridge between the book and people's everyday lives. One way to do this is by dangling a few intriguing questions in front of the congregation that will encourage them to start thinking seriously about some of the great issues of human existence that the book raises. This will also create some anticipation for what you will say in addressing these issues in the ensuing weeks. You can say something like this:

> The book of Job raises a number of profound and difficult questions about our existence as human beings. Each of you has already asked some of these questions yourself. You may not have a good answer to any of them, but they are important for us to ask because they help us understand the nature of our world and where we fit in. These are universal questions with which every generation of philosophers, theologians, writers, and artists has had to grapple. And we will do some more grappling with them in the weeks ahead.
>
> Here are some of the significant questions we will consider in the next several weeks:
> - What kind of God runs this universe? What adjectives would you use to describe him? Is he loving, kind, friendly, generous, and compassionate? Or is he powerful, frightening, mysterious, and vindictive?
> - Is God really concerned about justice? If so, why does he allow some good people to suffer tragedies and some bad people to avoid punishment?
> - Does God communicate with you on a regular basis, or are there long periods of silence? Does he respond to your questions and prayers with good answers? Or does he leave you in the dark much of the time?

Introduction

- What kind of a world do you live in? Is it a solid, stable world that operates according to dependable principles? Or is it a chaotic, insecure world where natural disasters and moral evil break in from time to time and disrupt your peaceful life?
- Is there someone in this world who is always trying to trip you up or test your faith in God? If so, what should/can you do about it?
- How should a person of faith react to unjust suffering? Is it OK to pour out your emotional hurts to God? Or should you always maintain a reserved, unemotional response?

We will look at all of these questions at some point in this series of sermons. By the end, you may not have any better answers than when we started. But at least you will know they are good, legitimate questions that need to be asked. And you will know that someone has already asked God these questions and struggled to find an answer, just as you have struggled.

The point of this introductory sermon is to make the congregation members feel they have been invited by their pastor to journey along together for a period of weeks in uncovering the meaning and application of this significant biblical book. They should be prepared to shake the cobwebs out of their thinking and engage with some of the great spiritual questions of all time. The effort may be difficult at times and may cause the shaking of the foundations of a person's faith, but it will be well worth the effort by helping people to grow into spiritual maturity.

Note to preachers: The material above could be combined with the next sermon into one sermon. But whether one sermon or two, it is important for the congregation to receive a good introduction to the book.

Possible Sermon Titles: "The Beginning of a Faith Journey," "A Timeless Book for Modern America," "A Timeless Book for Modern Times," "Journeying with Job"

I. JOB 1-2: PROLOGUE

Supersaint (Job 1:1-5)

The second sermon from Job should introduce the congregation to the main character of the story using 1:1-5. Who was Job, and why does that matter?

1. Job Was a Non-Israelite

The setting of the story and the characters involved in it were all non-Israelite. Job's name existed in other Semitic languages for hundreds of years before Hebrew was a spoken language. And the names of his three friends—Eliphaz, Bildad, and Zophar—were also non-Hebrew. Further, Job's place of residence and that of his friends were non-Israelite. Most scholars think that the region of Edom or northwestern Arabia was the most likely location of Uz (rhymes with "boots").

The reason this matters is because the author, even though he was Jewish, wanted his readers to understand that his book pertains to all humanity, not just the nation of Israel. Unjust suffering is a universal phenomenon. And the issues it raises have been discussed and debated by people of all time periods and cultures. Additionally, the reactions to unjust suffering by Job and his friends are typical reactions found in peoples all over the world.

2. Job's Relationship to God Was Ideal and Exemplary

In fact, it was better than that of any other character in the OT (including people such as Abraham, Moses, Samuel, David, and Isaiah). In 1:1 the author describes Job's spiritual characteristics using four outstanding attributes. He was "blameless and upright; he feared God and shunned evil" (the meaning of each of these attributes is expanded upon in detail in most commentaries). In other words, Job lived the kind of righteous life that was totally pleasing to God. Job was as ideal and holy as a finite human being could be. To further support the author's description here, God repeats the exact same words in verse 8 and 2:3.

3. Job Had an Ideal Family

While the size of his family was much larger than most families today, the ancient world would have regarded the number of Job's children as ideal. The number ten signified completeness. At the time of the story, Job's seven sons had all left home and were now living in their own houses. They probably had their own spouses and families, but these are not mentioned in the story. Job's three daughters were not yet married and thus still living at home, as was the custom in ancient times.

4. Job Had Phenomenal Wealth

Job owned hundreds of acres, where he farmed with his "five hundred yoke of oxen and five hundred donkeys" (1:3). But he also conducted business in distant places using servants and his "three thousand camels" (v. 3). Other servants were hired to shepherd his "seven thousand sheep" and goats as they migrated between summer and winter pastures (v. 3). In other words, Job was involved in several different moneymaking activities, both near and far away. He was one of the wealthiest persons of his day.

5. Job Regularly Interceded for Others

The welfare of Job's family was of prime importance to him. In 1:4-5 the author describes some regular family gatherings hosted by each of the seven sons. These were probably joyous birthday celebrations. Job did not attend, so he did not know exactly what transpired. But he was so concerned that one of his children might have done or said something sinful (perhaps carelessly or under the influence of alcohol [v. 13]) that he got up early in the morning following the feasts and offered a burnt offering for each of them. In other words, Job's piety as described in verse 1 was more than an internal exercise to strengthen his own faith. He also reached out to his family (v. 5) and friends (42:8), interceding for them with God.

I. Job 1-2: Prologue

John Wesley encouraged Christian parents to follow Job's example by praying for each of their children everyday (1765, 1518).

All in all, Job was ideal in so many ways that the author describes him as "the greatest man among all the people of the East" (1:3). And God later praises him with this statement: "There is no one on earth like him" (v. 8). Job had it all. He was exemplary in every respect. He was living the good life, according to the views of his culture.

What are we to take away from this impressive description of Job's character?

1. Job Was an Ideal Saint of God

He did not wear a blue shirt with a capital red "S" on the chest underneath his robe, but his character, deeds, thoughts, and attitudes were the godliest of any person in the OT. He was a holy person—a *supersaint*, praised both by the author and by God.

Job was also an extremely wise person (cf. 28:28 with 1:1). The book of Job is a part of the Wisdom Literature (also Proverbs, Ecclesiastes, and Song of Songs) that consistently praises wisdom as a supreme quality that everyone should seek with all their might (Prov. 3:13-18, 21-26; 4:5-9). Job was a hero to the sages of the ancient world.

It is vitally important that we understand the lofty pedestal upon which the author and God placed Job before we consider his losses. His fall into misery, poverty, grief, depression, and anger is even more striking when viewed against the heights of his ideal saintliness and wisdom in Job 1:1-5. No one has ever suddenly lost more than Job, because no person, with the exception of Jesus, has ever been as ideal as Job.

2. Job Possessed the Kind of Character That God Encourages Each of Us to Desire

What does that mean in practical terms? Does God want each family to have ten children? Obviously not.

Does God want all of us to strive for great wealth—to be the richest person in the world? Again, obviously not. God has created each of us with different talents and skills. And some of these skills are most useful in occupations that do not earn very much money.

Does God want people to seek after a great reputation? Good reputations are hard to come by, but easily lost. Most of us have little control over our reputations.

The answer to all three questions above is no! The most likely aspects of Job's life that God was pleased with were his godliness and his intercession for the spiritual well-being of others (also 42:8). These characteristics are praised in other parts of the Bible and could be expanded on here (godliness in Deut. 30:15-20; Josh. 1:7; Ps. 24:3-4; Matt. 5:8; 6:33; intercession in Gen. 18:23-33; 20:7, 17-18; 48:15-16; Exod. 32:11-14, 31-32; Num. 14:10-25; Pss. 25:22; 51:13 [15 HB]; Isa. 53:12; Dan. 9:17-19; Amos 7:1-6; Acts 12:5; 13:3; 1 Tim. 2:1-4; 1 John 5:16-17). These passages will help you define these two characteristics for your congregation (for a fuller discussion of intercession as one of the forms of prayer, see Miller 1994, 262-80).

The point of Job 1:1-5 is that Job was as ideal a human being as a person could be in the ancient world. As such, he provides a role model for all people of faith.

Here is a place where you can challenge your congregation to live lives of faith that exemplify Job's walk with God. What attitudes did he possess, and what actions did he undertake to prove that he was blameless and upright? How did he show that he feared God and shunned evil? This is not the place to construct a list of rules and regulations that set boundaries around righteous behavior. Rather, the congregation needs a description of how one man earned God's highest praise (v. 8) and how we can follow in his footsteps. Jesus offered guidelines for his followers in places such as the Sermon on the Mount (Matt. 5–7), and Paul did much the same in Galatians 5:22-23. Here are a few of Job's characteristics that could be emphasized:

- Complete loyalty to God in the face of personal suffering and tragedy (Job 1:21-22)
- Daily concern for his family's spiritual well-being (vv. 4-5)
- Generous support for the needy in his community (29:12-13, 15-16)

3. Job's Ideal Character and Behavior Did Not Prevent His Tragic Suffering

Job was doing everything right to the best of his ability, and yet he still experienced disease, loss, tragedy, and heartache. In other words, our level of faith and righteousness is not a determining factor in our level of suffering. The author wants the reader to know that even outstanding righteousness and wisdom do not prevent human suffering.

I. Job 1–2: Prologue

God has created the kind of world in which the troubles of life can interrupt anyone's journey at any time, no matter how hard he or she tries to avoid them. People may be able to prevent certain types of suffering through good choices and right living, but inevitably all people will experience some amount of suffering at some point in their lives. There is nothing we can do to prevent it. That should be a forewarning to us that we better make preparations for its arrival. And it also should be a caution not to judge those around us who are suffering. They may be as innocent as Job.

Possible Sermon Titles: "A Godly Role Model," "Meet the Old Testament's Supersaint," "How Does One Become a Supersaint?"

Reasons for Serving God (Job 1:6-12; 2:9)

In this section the author takes us into the courts of heaven for one of the most intriguing dialogues in all literary accounts of divine conversation. God and a new character with the title of "the Satan" (see 1:6) are discussing the reason for Job's outstanding righteousness (the word "Satan" always appears in Job with the definite article "the" on the front, indicating that it is not a proper name but a title describing his role as an adversary or an examiner). Does Job serve God because God is the Creator and he deserves humanity's worship and obedience? Or does Job serve God because God has blessed him abundantly and he wants this treatment to continue?

The basic question is, What is Job's motivation for serving God? Everyone agrees he is the most outstanding example of righteousness in his generation. But why is he this way? What motivates him to live like a supersaint? Does he get something back out of it, such as a reward, that encourages him to keep living this way?

Before going any further with a discussion of the heavenly conversation, it is important to define the character named "the Satan." The immediate congregational response to this term is negative, for it is used repeatedly in the NT with regard to "a demonic, personal source of evil who does everything he can to destroy God's kingdom" (Bowes 2018, 48). But the word does not have this meaning in the OT. There it refers to a variety of human as well as divine characters who were adversaries of someone (e.g., the Philistines were afraid that David would become their satan/adversary [1 Sam. 29:4]).

I. Job 1-2: Prologue

In the book of Job the author wants us to understand that the character who dialogues with God in the prologue is not demonic. He is one of the angels, and God has given him the task of examining and questioning the validity of people's claims of piety. "Testing people is his job" (Reyburn 1992, 39). And Job has raised the Satan's suspicions that Job's righteous character is too good to be true. For this reason, in my commentary I used the title "the Examiner" instead of "the Satan" because it describes much better the role he plays in Job (for a more detailed discussion of my usage of the term "Examiner," see Bowes 2018, 47-50).

The question the Examiner raises with God is brief but powerful: "Does Job fear God for nothing?" (1:9). This is a skeptical question implying that Job is not really a supersaint after all. He may look like one on the outside, but deep in his heart he craves the many rewards that God bestows on those who serve him—things such as wealth, an ideal family, and protection from danger and harm.

The Examiner then challenges God to test whether his theory is correct or not: "God, remove the rewards from Job's life, and then we will know what really motivates him to serve you!" God seems intrigued by this challenge. And maybe he also recognizes the logic of the Examiner's argument. In any case, he permits the Examiner to conduct a test that will reveal the real reason why Job serves God.

The Examiner is not placing a bet here. He is simply asking God to *test* Job as a way of proving his suspicion that Job is a religious phony. This test is similar to God's test of Abraham (Gen. 22:1-19). In both cases, God wanted to know whether these men truly trusted him with their whole being and without benefit of a reward or a threat of loss.

Once you have gotten to the heart of the issue, you can make application to the congregation. "If you claim to be a person of faith, a follower of Christ, why do you serve God? What would the Examiner find in a test of your faith?" And even more broadly: "Is all religion basically self-centered? Do people serve God mainly because they get something out of it and/or feel threatened with punishment if they do not?" Blackwood puts the question this way: "Do we worship God for the trinkets that fall from His hand, or for the sake of God alone?" (1959, 89).

Do you believe that if you serve God, he will give you a great spouse, a nice family, a profitable job, all the necessities of life, and an early retirement? And if you do not serve God, you will experience the opposite—conflict in your marriage, kids that embarrass you, a job that you

I. Job 1-2: Prologue

hate and pays little, and so forth? Do you believe that if you serve God, you will have good health? And if you do not serve God, you will likely end up with cancer or a heart attack?

All of these questions speak to the issue of the consequences that one experiences by serving God. What expectations do you have about what will happen to you if you are obedient to God's will for your life?

These are not unreasonable questions, because most of the people in the world from time immemorial have believed that our choices in life have consequences. We will discover as we make our way through this book that Job believes this, his wife believes it, his three friends believe it, a young person named Elihu believes it, and most of the rest of the OT believes it. For example, see Moses's speech to the Israelites in Deut. 30:15-20. "Serve God and you will be blessed; disobey God and you will be punished" is a standard OT theme. It is all black and white. The entire book of Proverbs supports this concept.

And most of us would agree initially with the Examiner. There has to be some kind of reward associated with the things we do, or we would not do them. How many people would go to work if they were not rewarded with a paycheck? Who would go to school if they were not rewarded with a degree or graduation certificate and the ability to make a higher salary and a better living? Who would get married if they were not rewarded with intimacy and companionship and children? Who would pay their taxes if not threatened with the possibility of a fine or jail time? We live in a world of rewards and punishments. We understand this world very well. So the Examiner's question seems to be very rational and truthful.

However, is this the way God intended for religion to work? God believes not, and this is why he allows the test to take place—to prove to the Examiner and to all who read this book that people do not need the promise of rewards or the threat of punishment to make a decision to serve God. A person can decide to serve God for better reasons than rewards, for example, simply because he is the creator of all things and deserves our obedience, or because he is the only one able to forgive our sins and remove our guilt.

In Job 2:9, Job's wife appears. She clearly believed, like the Examiner, that rewards were a basic part of religion. Her husband, Job, should have been blessed by God, because she knew he had been very righteous. As his wife, she enjoyed some of the same rewards that he did—an ideal family, tremendous wealth, good health, and so forth. But things have changed now. Their children were all dead, their livelihood was gone, and Job's health was so bad he could no longer work. Clearly, her husband was not being blessed by God anymore. She assumed he was being punished. So why should Job continue to maintain his faith in God? It had gotten him absolutely nothing but heartaches and suffering. In her mind it was pointless to serve God any longer because apparently there was no connection between obedience and rewards, although she thought there should have been. Most people in the ancient world would have agreed with her.

Many of us fall into the same misunderstanding that Job's wife experienced. We expect God to bless us whenever we are obedient, and we cannot figure out why life sometimes goes badly for us, even though we are serving God to the best of our abilities.

What's the answer to this most difficult issue? Over the centuries people have proposed many solutions to this problem. And the book of Job enumerates some of the better-known ones.

Some, like Job's three friends whom we will meet shortly (2:11-13), have tried to maintain the principle of rewards by suggesting that Job was not really a supersaint. He had some secret sin(s) in his life that he refused to admit or had long forgotten. Maybe Job had done something really bad as a teenager that now was coming back to bite him. Job was willing to admit this possibility if someone would just tell him what this sin was (13:26). But the reader knows that this is impossible. The prologue makes it absolutely clear that both the author and God believed Job was a supersaint. There was no sin in his life at the beginning of the book. "This man was blameless and upright; he feared God and shunned evil" (1:1).

Other people have noted that no human being is perfect in character (5:7). Every one of us has messed up at some point in life. Job must have forgotten his times of failure. It is true that human beings are imperfect, but this does not explain Job's terrible suffering.

Still others have suggested that sometimes we experience the consequences of other people's sins. Perhaps Job's children's sins had fallen on him (8:4). Again, the reader knows that Job's troubles were not caused by his children.

And further, some people have argued that even if Job was perfectly righteous, he still should expect some amount of suffering in his life, for

I. Job 1–2: Prologue

God uses suffering to discipline us for our own good (5:17). Yes, he does, but Job was not in need of such discipline.

The answer the author provides to the question, Why do people serve God? is not an essay on the merits of faith without rewards. Rather, it is the life story of a man named Job whose struggles with this question proved once and for all that human beings can serve God "for nothing" (1:9). The Examiner was wrong and God was right, and all heaven and earth are now privy to this information. All people may not be able to demonstrate the same courageous faith as Job. They may crack under the stresses and losses that Job experienced. But Job proved that faith in God can be maintained without rewards and in spite of horrendous losses. This is a great lesson to keep in mind as we continue along on our own journey through life. God is worthy of our obedience and service even if we never receive a single reward.

Possible Sermon Titles: "Serve God for Nothing?" "Is God Obligated to Bless You When You Serve Him?" "What Is the Real Reason Why People Should Serve God?" "When It Does Not Pay to Serve God, What Are We to Do?" "How Does God Bless His Followers?"

When Life Goes Topsy-Turvy (Job 1:13-22; 2:7-8)

The pain Job endured came from a variety of sources. Some was caused by what we often call natural disasters. Lightning struck his sheep, and a great windstorm killed his ten children. But people in the ancient world did not think of disasters as natural. And many people around the world today do not either. They see disasters as a form of divine punishment.

Some of Job's pain was inflicted by other people who desired to do him harm. The Sabeans and Chaldeans, two ethnic groups who lived hundreds of miles away, suddenly appeared out of nowhere and seized Job's camels, donkeys, and oxen.

And then a mysterious skin disease began to ravage Job's body. Ancient people did not understand disease at all. They had no knowledge of deadly bacteria and viruses. They thought disease was of supernatural origin, caused either by one of the gods or by demons from the underworld.

In our world today, we experience the same types of suffering from natural disasters, disease, and harm inflicted by other people. We go about our daily lives enjoying our families, our work, and our material

I. Job 1–2: Prologue

possessions, when suddenly our world is shattered by an unforeseen event such as a diagnosis of cancer or dementia, the onset of debilitating back pain, a home burglary, a car accident, or identity theft (you can add to this list based on the experiences of your parishioners). Suddenly we feel vulnerable and helpless in ways we never felt before. Life seems so fragile and short.

We stop to consider the causes and think about ways to avoid this from happening again. Maybe we should not have purchased that pretty little cabin in the woods surrounded by all those dry trees. Maybe we should not have been texting while driving. Maybe we should have given up cigarettes and alcohol and spent more time exercising instead of watching TV. Maybe it is time to hire a company to monitor our credit accounts.

Job probably did some second-guessing about how he might have avoided trouble: "I should have stationed guards with my shepherds and servants. Or I should have moved my sheep to a different pasture. Or I should have told my servants in charge of the camels to follow a different route." But the fact is that no one can completely protect himself or herself from all the possible dangers in life. Cancer strikes people at all ages. Car accidents happen even to people who seldom drive. Natural disasters affect everyone in their paths. And even the dead can have their identities stolen.

And further, we do not know if it is true or not, but if it is true that God assigns an Examiner to test each person's faith, there is no way we can avoid these kinds of calamities, for the Examiner is one individual who really knows how to hurt a person in testing that person's faith.

Thus, if trouble is inevitably going to affect each of us, there is only one question that remains to be answered. How are we going to let suffering affect us? What is it going to do to our emotions, to our sense of well-being and self-worth, to our relationships with other people, and to our relationship with God?

Here is where the book of Job gives us different options. In chapter 3, Job lets loose a series of awful curses. They are so bad they make the ears tingle. His physical body is racked with pain, his mind is reeling over the destruction of his livelihood, and his heart is grieving over the loss of his children. He sees absolutely nothing good happening in his life, and the only way to relieve his anguish is to curse. Only in this case, the curse is against himself, specifically his birth date. He wishes he had never been born so that he could have avoided so much pain.

In chapters 1 and 2, Job has a completely different reaction. He seems to be cool, calm, and collected when he says in 1:21: "The LORD gave and the LORD has taken away; may the name of the LORD be praised." This has caused commentators a great deal of anguish in trying to reconcile the two reactions. Who is the real Job? How can one person change so radically between chapters 2 and 3? A number of attempts have been made to resolve this issue, but none are completely satisfactory (see Bowes 2018, 59-60).

What we can and should say is that at this point in the narrative Job is acknowledging God's right as Creator to do as he wishes with each of our lives. He does this by comparing the beginning and ending of life to nakedness. We enter this life with none of this world's goods, and we leave it in the same way. It is as if we are naked at both ends of our fourscore years. The ancient pharaohs of Egypt did not believe this, for they filled their tombs with golden thrones, chariots, household goods, and weapons—things that might be needed in the afterlife. But the biblical belief is that none of the accumulated treasures of life can be carried into the next world (1 Tim. 6:7).

However, we do accumulate some quantity of material things between birth and death. Job, as well as the rest of the Bible, viewed these items as gifts from God. It is true that God may give some of them as rewards for our service, but we all are blessed far more than we deserve. For this reason, most of our rewards should be viewed as evidence of God's love and grace. We should be thankful for God's gifts while we have them. But we should not hold them too tightly, for God may choose to take them back from us at any time. But whether we are naked or clothed in the richest garments this world has to offer, God is always worthy of our praise.

When things go wrong in people's lives, there is always the temptation to assign blame. Somehow it makes us feel better if we can identify the source of our troubles. And once the evil culprits are known, there is an intense desire for justice to be imposed. But Job did not play that game. He could easily have pronounced terrible curses on the Sabeans and Chaldeans, for he knew their names. Or he could have cursed God for causing the freakish weather phenomena that took his children and sheep.

Instead, Job simply acknowledged that God was the ultimate cause of his calamities. "The severity, the totality, and the suddenness of his losses" were not just a coincidence (Bowes 2018, 58). He knew they pointed directly back to God.

In later speeches Job cried out to God for an explanation of these disasters. We would probably do the same. *Why* is a very common human response to misfortune. But at this point in the narrative, Job was too stunned to question God about his motives. All his prior religious training and practice kicked in. All he knew to do was to acknowledge God's right as Creator to do whatever he wished with his creation and then to praise his name for his goodness.

Job had certainly been the recipient of God's goodness many times before. Now he recognized, maybe for the first time, that God also sometimes takes away. But the latter did not negate the former. It just made it more difficult to maintain one's faith and avoid "charging God with wrongdoing" (Job 1:22).

Two important observations arise from this passage. The first is that at some point, life will go topsy-turvy for each of us. It is inevitable. Bad stuff happens. And our stuff may not have anything to do with retributive justice or corrective discipline. As the prologue makes clear, Job's calamities were not the result of sin, either his own or someone else's. The second is that our reaction to life's troubles reveals the quality and depth of our faith—our "integrity" (2:9). How will we let suffering affect us?

It is not wrong to express our pain and grief in emotional ways. It is not wrong to seek the reason why, although we should recognize that we may never get a good answer. It is not wrong to believe that we are innocent sufferers. It is not even wrong to question God for allowing trouble to happen. But it is wrong to accuse God of injustice. And it is wrong to withhold our praise of him. We will find support for these concepts in other parts of the book, but certainly 1:21-22 provides the first opportunity to reflect on the impact of suffering on faith.

Possible Sermon Titles: "How to Really Hurt a Guy," "Living in the Light of Our Nakedness," "Who's to Blame?" "A Really Bad-Hair Day in the Life of a Saint," "Real Life Hurts Sometimes," "Lessons Learned the Hard Way"

I. Job 1-2: Prologue

"The Lord Gave . . . the Lord Has Taken Away" (Job 2:1-10)

What would it take to get you to give up your faith in God? Would the sudden loss of your possessions and children be enough to turn your heart away from God? The Examiner had been convinced that this would change Job's relationship with God. But he was mistaken. Job had survived the first onslaught of calamities with flying colors. He believed that God was ultimately responsible for all of these losses. But he also knew that God could do whatever he wished with his creatures. Consequently, Job had no reason to blame God, even when things went very badly for him (1:21).

However, the Examiner was not done trying to test the motivation for Job's faith. He had one more calamity to inflict. He was now convinced that Job's health was the key. So he went to God to request a further extension of his trials against God's most outstanding saint. God was already upset at the amount of suffering his servant was enduring. He scolded the Examiner for inflicting all of this pain "without any reason" (2:3). The initial test had been a failure, and God seemed to be interested in ending it quickly. But the Examiner pressed God to allow another test. He believed that an attack against Job's health would force Job to fear his own death. And such a fear would cause him to curse God and sever his relationship with the Almighty.

"Skin for skin!" (v. 4) are the Examiner's exact words to God. The meaning of this phrase is open to debate, but it seems to be an ancient proverb that buyers and sellers used in bartering over the sale of commodities in the marketplace. The Examiner thought that if Job was afflicted with a disease he thought was terminal, he would start bargaining for his life. He would be willing to exchange his faith in God for healing from this disease.

The point the Examiner was trying to make with God is that all human beings are self-centered. They are only interested in their own well-being. Any praise they bestow on God is given with the expectation of a reward. We saw this same argument back in 1:6-12, but the Examiner takes it a step further in 2:4. Here the thought is not on a reward, but rather on avoiding pain. Physical pain is something humans seek to avoid at all costs. They will give up about anything to rid themselves of a painful disease and the possibility of death.

I. Job 1–2: Prologue

God knew that the Examiner had a valid point, for some people respond to disease with bitterness and cursing. No doubt, he was alarmed that his servant Job would have to endure more suffering, but he wanted all heaven and earth to be convinced that a relationship with God is not dependent on rewards or the avoidance of pain. People can and do serve God in spite of losses and severe suffering. God believed that Job was just the person to prove his point, and so he allowed the Examiner to proceed with a second test.

The exact name of the disease Job experienced is unknown, but we know several things about it. It was a skin disease that covered his entire body. It was very painful to him and awful looking to others. It oozed pus and itched terribly. There was no known cure. And significantly, this disease was associated with the anger of God (cf. Exod. 9:9-11; Deut. 28:27, 35; and see Bowes 2018, 64-65), so there were spiritual implications of which Job and his friends were aware.

This created a terrible conflict in Job's mind. He knew he looked like the worst of sinners who was being punished by God. No one wanted to be around him. Even his wife only came to see him briefly. But yet he also believed he was in a right relationship with God. How could both of these things be true? The test of Job's faith here is exactly the kind of extreme test the Examiner had in mind when he asked God to take away Job's health.

In an earlier sermon (→ "Reasons for Serving God," p. 27), we commented on the appearance of Job's wife in Job 2:9. Her purpose was mainly to raise the question *why*. "Why are you still loyal to God when he has punished us so severely?" Job's answer in verse 10 deserves some careful attention.

First, he accuses his wife of "talking like a foolish woman" (v. 10). The word "foolish" is a very common word in all of the Wisdom Literature. It usually refers to a person who is lacking in wisdom and knowledge about the important issues of life. This condition is not caused by a lack of intelligence, but rather by a self-centered attitude that rejects God and his will (Prov. 1:7). Foolish people are not totally wicked, but they are morally corrupt. They fill their minds with folly. They refuse to learn from their mistakes because they think they are always right. And their hardheaded attitude and quarrelsome nature often lead to conflict with family and friends (for more on the characteristics of a fool, see Kidner 1964, 39-42).

I. Job 1–2: Prologue

In general, the Wisdom Literature bemoans the overall foolishness of the world's population, while praising the few who follow the instructions of God and Lady Wisdom (Prov. 1:20-33; 8:1-36; 9:1-6). Too many people reject God and the way of wisdom. Job's comment to his wife in Job 2:10 is intended to point out her foolishness and direct her toward an attitude and a lifestyle that faithfully honor God and his plans for the world.

Job's second comment ("Shall we accept good from God, and not trouble?" [v. 10*b*]) is a rhetorical question that encourages her (and all of us) to accept that both good and bad will happen to us in this life. The words "good" and "trouble" are polar opposites. They indicate the extremes at either end of the spectrum of life's events. And they include everything in between—all the mundane, mediocre things that occur on most normal days.

Job's words here are a powerful indictment against those who practice the gospel of success (prosperity gospel). Some think that people who worship God with all their heart will avoid the major troubles of life and succeed in all their endeavors. We will see in later chapters that Job's friends had just such a belief. But Job's words to his wife in verse 10 clearly indicate that such is not the case. No one is immune from life's troubles. Calamity, sickness, betrayal, harm, and natural disasters happen to all people, no matter how faithful they are to God. Anything (both good and bad) can happen to anyone at any time.

In verse 10 there is an important word that needs clarification. It is the word translated as "accept" (NIV) or "receive" (NRSV). There are different attitudes one can take toward the troubles of life. One is that of resignation or submission. This is the attitude of the slave who must obey the master's commands without complaint. Another attitude is that of the stoic who grits his or her teeth and struggles through life's hardships without emotion. A third attitude is that of bitterness, even accompanied with thoughts of revenge.

However, none of these are what Job had in mind. Job wanted his wife to accept their troubles with a sense of humbleness toward God. God had blessed them abundantly in previous years ("the LORD gave" [1:21]), and now he had chosen to bring trouble into their lives ("the LORD has taken away" [v. 21]). Neither of them knew why God had done this, and maybe they would never know the reason. But that should not hinder their devotion and praise to God. Even without a good explanation, they could still trust in God and believe he knew best about the course of their lives. We will be reminded of this concept again when we get to God's speeches at the end of the book.

So, what would it take to get you to give up your faith in God? Hopefully, the answer is nothing. Hopefully, you can testify with Paul "that neither death nor life, neither angels nor demons, neither the present nor the future, nor any powers, neither height nor depth, nor anything else in all creation, will be able to separate us from the love of God that is in Christ Jesus our Lord" (Rom. 8:38-39).

Possible Sermon Titles: "Skin for Skin!" "What Would It Take . . . ?" "God's Guinea Pigs," "God Knows Best?"

Friends (Job 2:11-13)

The action in the prologue is now finished. The author has told us that Job was living the life of a supersaint at the beginning of the story. He then describes a debate in heaven between God and a divine character who acts as his Examiner. They both agree that Job is an extremely righteous person, but they part company over the reasons for Job's piety. The Examiner thinks Job is only righteous because of the rewards it brings him, such as an ideal family and enormous wealth. But God believes that Job has chosen to live righteously for more noble and spiritual reasons. To prove he is right, God permits the Examiner to remove Job's family, possessions, and health. The stage is now set for the reader to view Job's reactions to his suffering. Will he give up his faith in God when the rewards are taken away?

The immediate answer, as given in the prologue, is no. As we noted in the previous two sermons, Job makes some very positive comments that seem to indicate he has a solid faith in God based on a personal relationship (1:21; 2:10). His faith cannot be shaken. But we will learn in chapter 3 that Job's faith has been shaken to its very core. He believes that God is treating him like the worst of sinners, and he cannot understand why. He needs some explanation from God to help him through this series of crises.

The two main heavenly characters now disappear from the story. The Examiner, who had inflicted terrible pain on Job, leaves for good. His theory that Job was motivated to serve God by the promise of rewards has been proven wrong. God also disappears, but he will reappear near the end of the book.

I. Job 1-2: Prologue

In the meantime, the author presents us with an extended dialogue between Job and three friends from former days—"Eliphaz," "Bildad," and "Zophar" (2:11). These names are connected with the period of the patriarchs in the book of Genesis (see Bowes 2018, 71-73), but no direct connection has been established with any specific person in Genesis. Most likely, the author was simply trying to provide a setting for the narrative in a foreign land in an ancient time prior to the nation of Israel.

Apparently, Job had established a relationship with these friends at some time in the past, but they now lived at some distance from him in different towns. When they received the news that their old friend Job was seriously ill and had suffered some terrible losses, they decided to visit him for the purpose of consoling him. They made arrangements to meet together at a certain location, and then they traveled as a group to the town of Uz.

They were aghast at Job's appearance. They did not even recognize him when they first saw him outside the city sitting on the refuse at the town garbage dump. They would become even more alarmed when they heard him speak. This was not the same old Job.

Verses 11-13 are intended to be a very brief transition into the main part of the book. The author gives us very few details about the three friends, other than the location from where they came. But we will learn much more about them as the book unfolds, for they each have extended speeches in the next twenty-five chapters.

It is in these speeches that we come to recognize three different personalities. One is gentle and mystical. One is a traditionalist. And the third is a dogmatist. Each will contribute something unique to the dialogue. But the three friends have one thing in common. They all think of themselves as very wise. They see themselves as sages, and they believe they are experts on the subject of suffering.

There was already a great deal of literature in the ancient world on this topic. People had studied it and had written about it for hundreds of years prior to the book of Job. So there was already a long tradition of knowledge that the three friends could draw upon. They claimed to know this wisdom tradition very well.

We do not know the ages of these three men, but one passage (15:10) hints that they were older gentlemen, perhaps as old as Job's father. Age in the ancient world was respected for its wisdom. Thus these men had age on their side as well as a long tradition of observation of human life and the natural world.

There are a number of commendable qualities about these three friends. For one, they showed up when Job desperately needed a friend to talk to. No one else among Job's relatives or neighbors ventured to even get close to him.

For another, they empathized with his anguish. They wept, they tore their robes, and they sprinkled dust on their heads—all signs of grief. They showed by these actions that they shared his deep distress over his losses.

And then the text indicates that their purpose in coming was to console Job. It was not to criticize or to gain tidbits of gossip for when they returned home. They truly wanted to help this poor soul who needed comfort.

And finally, they remained silent out of respect for their old friend Job. They wanted to allow him some time to process his grief, and they needed to hear him speak before they jumped in with their own evaluation of his situation. So they held their tongues for seven days until Job erupted with a very emotional, distraught outburst that revealed the tremendous physical, mental, and spiritual pain he was experiencing.

Before we get to that speech in chapter 3, it is important to consider the meaning of the term "friends" that is applied to them in 2:11. What is a friend? Do these three individuals deserve to be called friends? Or are they the kind of people who are mentioned in our English proverb "With friends like these, who needs enemies?" Knowing the definition of a true friend should be important to those who want to be one.

The book of Proverbs attempts to define the concept of friendship. It contains numerous admonitions to help people in choosing good friends and in being a good friend/neighbor to someone else. Kidner (1964, 44-46) has summarized the characteristics of a good friend in the book of Proverbs under four headings: (1) good friends are always there when you need them; (2) good friends are candid in their advice; (3) good friends offer counsel that is appropriate for the situation; and (4) good friends are tactful when counseling with someone in need. Kidner's book (or other commentaries on Proverbs) would be very helpful in defining for your congregation what it means to be a good friend.

Balentine defines a true friend as one who brings two things to a relationship: "loyalty" and "companionship" (2006, 142-43). By loyalty he means "that friends will not let go of friends no matter what. In good times and bad, in success and failure, in joy and in sorrow, friends should be present with equal commitment and passion" (142). Companionship refers to a willingness to actually be in the presence of someone who is suffering. Too many times people withdraw from those who are experiencing some type of trouble. A true friend knows that just being there in a time of crisis is worth more to the sufferer than any words that can be spoken. Companionship may not "ease the pain," but it "improve[s] the quality of suffering" (143).

How did Eliphaz, Bildad, and Zophar live up to these definitions of a friend provided by Kidner and Balentine? At this point in the story, they seem to be doing very well. They took time out of their schedule to visit Job, and their purpose in coming was to console. But we will discover very quickly that they were too full of themselves. Their insistence that they were the only ones who understood Job's situation soon turned Job against them.

We will have numerous opportunities as we study their speeches to note their failure at being good counselors. Job needed their help desperately. But they let their image of themselves get in the way of being good friends. When people think they have the truth on their side, they sometimes fall prey to an attitude of haughtiness or arrogance that prevents honest dialogue and respect for the views of others.

Like Job, we also wish that friends would show up when we are overwhelmed by the troubles of life. We usually welcome with open arms anyone who attempts to be a friend in our times of need. The presence of a true friend who deeply cares about us is an indescribable blessing. It is much better to establish these relationships ahead of time than to have to generate them after the fact.

The conclusion to this sermon might be a personal example of a friend who has meant a great deal to you over the years or a biblical example such as the relationship between David and Jonathan or Jeremiah and Baruch.

At the end of this sermon, it would be a good idea to prepare the congregation for the change in subject matter in the chapters that follow. Job's verbal responses in 1:21 and 2:10 clearly indicate that he was not going to let calamity, no matter how severe, interrupt his relationship with God. The Examiner's theory that faith in God was dependent on rewards or the threat of punishment had been proven totally wrong.

I. Job 1–2: Prologue

So the author raises some new questions in the remainder of the book through the speeches of the friends. Why was Job suffering? Who or what had caused his pain? And how could he be restored? What did he need to do to regain his health, his wealth, and his family?

The friends' appearance at this point leads to this new topic. They will present the best thinking available that the wisdom traditions had to offer. But they will fail miserably in their attempts to provide the solution to Job's problems. We need to listen carefully to their arguments lest we, too, make a similar mistake.

Possible Sermon Titles: "A Friend in Need Is a Friend Indeed," "The Influences of Other People on Our Faith," "The Importance of Good Friends along Life's Journey," "With Friends like These . . ."

II. JOB 3: JOB'S ANGUISH

Dealing with Bitterness (Job 3)

Few sermons have ever been preached from chapter 3. The reason is obvious. The tone of the whole chapter is one of gloom and despair. Job is very distraught after suffering terrible losses in chapters 1–2. He sees nothing positive in his future. Death is the only recourse that will free him from his misery. He wishes it would come immediately and whisk him off to Sheol, the place of the dead. Or better yet, he wishes he had never been born. So chapter 3 is difficult to preach from, but not impossible. One must just work a little harder to understand its context and make applications to a contemporary congregation.

In chapter 3 we discover for the first time how deeply Job is hurting inside. All of his pent-up emotions that were kept in check in chapters 1–2 suddenly explode in a loud outburst of cursing and anger as well as fear and dread. This raises the issue of Job's emotional stability. How could a person go so quickly from his strong words of faith in 1:21 to an intense desire to die in chapter 3? Job almost seems like two different people. We will come back to this issue later.

An appropriate way to begin this sermon would be to describe all of the raw emotions that Job expresses in this chapter and what this indicates about his thinking at this point. He has now suffered for some time—physically, mentally, and emotionally. He spends his days at the town garbage dump, scratching the painful sores/boils on his skin with broken pieces of pottery. He has no sense of self-worth anymore. All the things that gave his life meaning and value and established his sterling reputation in his community were now gone—his occupation, his compassionate works, his wealth, and his family. Even his wife, whom

II. Job 3: Job's Anguish

he depended on in the past, misunderstood his anguish. Her words were foolish and seemed unsympathetic.

When Job's friends arrived, they were probably expecting some words from him like those he uttered in 1:21 and 2:10, for their previous encounters with him had revealed a person who understood the true meaning of life and spoke with great wisdom. Thus they were shocked at what they heard coming from his mouth in chapter 3.

Job's first words were a curse against his birth date that then led into repeated regrets that he had been born. Why did he ever exist? He wished it had never happened. He focuses his regrets on the events surrounding his birth.

First, he wished he had never been conceived or born (vv. 1-10). Using skillful poetic imagery, he describes a series of scenarios that would have prevented his birth: (1) If the day of his birth or the night of his conception had been removed from the calendar, he would never have been born. (2) If light had never shown on his birth date, if the sun had never come up, then darkness would have prevailed and kept him from ever seeing the light. (3) If skilled sorcerers had been hired to pronounce a curse against his birth date, then chaos would have broken out and prevented his birth from taking place. (4) Or if the doors of his mother's womb had been shut so that his father's semen could not enter her uterus, then his conception would never have occurred.

The whole point of this argument is that God failed to do any of these things, which he could have done if he had wanted. Therefore, God was responsible for causing Job's entrance into a life of misery that Job now wished had never begun.

Have you ever felt that God failed to intervene in a situation that was headed for disaster? Have you ever asked God questions such as these: "Why didn't you prevent that disease from claiming my spouse?" "Why didn't you prevent that drunk driver from going the wrong way on the interstate highway?" "Why didn't you steer that hurricane out into the ocean instead of allowing it to devastate a populated area?" How did that make you feel toward God when he failed to intervene, and you suffered as a result? People who experience these kinds of tragedies know exactly how Job felt in chapter 3.

Second, Job moves a step further in verses 11-19. Even if none of the above events had occurred, Job still could have avoided his anguish if he had perished at birth or been stillborn. When he exited his mother's

II. Job 3: Job's Anguish

womb, why were there parents and a midwife there to welcome him into this world? Why had these people begun to feed him and clothe him and show him attention? If no one had done these things, he would have died within a few days of birth and thus avoided his miserable life. But again, God had failed to prevent his birth. God must have wanted him to endure an awful existence.

Third, why does God do this to people? Why does he cause human beings to be born when he knows they will come to hate their lives and wish to exit this world into Sheol? Here (vv. 20-26) Job broadens his complaint to include all of humanity. He had observed so many people who were in misery just as he was. They had no peace or rest. They groaned constantly. They had become bitter at what life had brought them. And they did not desire to live any longer because they saw no purpose or meaningful future for themselves. It was as if God had placed them in a great corn maze. They were lost and could not find their way out. God had hedged them in. What was God's purpose in doing this?

Job's words in this chapter are some of the most depressing and bitter in the entire Bible. How could people become so devoid of hope that they wished they had never been born? These words shock us just as much as they shocked the three friends. But the friends needed to hear Job's ranting before offering their advice. They could not help him without first knowing his heart. Listening is an essential part of good counseling and building friendships.

To understand this passage, one needs to have some knowledge of the Hebrew conception of the afterlife, since the concept is so much different than that found in the NT. The Hebrew word for the afterlife is *Sheol*. This word does not appear in this chapter, but it is implied in verses 13-15 and 17-19, and it is found in eight other passages in the book (7:9; 11:8; 14:13; 17:13, 16; 21:13; 24:19; 26:6; some versions prefer the translation "grave" rather than "Sheol"). No single passage in the OT provides a complete definition of Sheol, so a number of texts are needed to gain an understanding. Psalm 88 is especially helpful (see others in Bowes 2018, 86-87).

Generally speaking, Sheol was the place of the dead, a place of separation from God deep under the ground ("the pit" [Job 33:18, 24, 28, 30]). The shades/individuals who inhabited it did not experience God's steadfast love, and so they had no reason to praise him. Everyone went to Sheol, from "the small" to "the great," from "the wicked" to the righteous

(3:17, 19). In other words, rewards and punishments were not handed out to those who had died and were now in Sheol.

In addition, Sheol was a place where social conflicts between people no longer existed, according to chapter 3. There was "peace," "quietness," and "rest" in Sheol (vv. 13, 17, 26). This is what attracted Job to thinking about Sheol and wishing he could go there. He believed that all of his emotional turmoil would end once he exited this world.

At this point in the sermon, you will need to make a choice about where to go from here and how to provide a suitable application for a contemporary congregation. Here are four options from which to choose.

1. A NT Understanding of the Afterlife

The discussion of Sheol opens the door to describing how the NT conception of heaven and hell is so much different. The OT is not the final word on the afterlife. The NT provides a more satisfying conclusion to life on this earth. What are the ways in which it is better? What hope does Christ give to the person who is facing death? Here one would need to develop the descriptions of heaven given in such passages as Matthew 24–25; John 14; 1 Thessalonians 4:13–5:11; 2 Thessalonians 1:3–2:12; and the book of Revelation.

2. Restoring Wholeness in Times of Great Loss

There is no question that there was a radical change in Job's attitude between 1:21 and chapter 3. How could this happen (for more discussion, see Bowes 2018, 90-91)? Does chapter 3 indicate a backslidden state in Job's spiritual condition? Does it indicate a new stage in his processing of grief over the death of his children? Is this chapter simply a literary device to give the three friends an awareness of Job's feelings and thus something to react to? Or is the author attempting in chapter 3 to show all the contrasting emotions Job was wrestling with internally?

Job seems to be very emotional in this chapter, and yet his emotions are typical expressions of anger and bitterness that normal human beings feel when confronted with horrendous loss. Here preachers have the opportunity to talk about human nature, emotional ups and downs, and spiritual growth. Are our emotions different from or similar to Job's? What are normal and what are abnormal emotions for the Christian?

Newsom, borrowing from Dorothee Soelle (*Suffering*, trans. E. Kalin [Philadelphia: Fortress, 1975], 68-74), has an enlightening essay on the

II. Job 3: Job's Anguish

"phases of suffering" that troubled people go through to reach wholeness again (1996, 371-72). She identifies these phases as "mute suffering," "speaking suffering," and "changing."

In the first phase, people turn inward and suffer silently. They avoid speaking as they attempt to resolve the pain of their crisis inwardly. Job's "seven days and seven nights" (2:13) of silence were his initial way of dealing with his sorrow.

In the second phase, sufferers attempt to give voice to their pain. Speaking about it helps to relieve the feeling of helplessness. But the words are not always expressed in typical Christian language. They may be laced with anger, blame, and bitterness, even against God. And this may frighten friends who come to console. Job's friends were certainly disturbed over his emotional outbursts. But this speaking phase had to take place before healing could occur.

In the third phase, sufferers experience major internal changes that enable them to move past their grief and anger and focus their energies in positive, constructive ways. This is "a phase in which active behavior is possible, objectives can be identified, and solidarity with other persons forms new community" (Newsom 1996, 372).

In Job's case the third phase did not begin until God appeared and began to show Job how the creation itself revealed his deep concern for every part of the universe (chs. 38–41). Then Job realized that God cared for him too. God was not really the enemy he had imagined earlier. Rather, God was the best friend he could ever hope for. Once Job had achieved reconciliation with God (42:6), then his attitude toward life changed. His support system of family and friends reemerged (v. 11), his means of financial support returned (vv. 10, 12), and he took up his old practice of ministering to others (1:5; 42:9).

There is one final question: What does this chapter reveal about God's acceptance of our emotional ups and downs and our outbursts in prayer? Do we need to put aside our emotional human nature when conversing with God? For additional passages on this subject, see the confessions of Jeremiah (Jer. 8:18–9:2; 11:18-20; 12:1-6; 15:10-12, 15-21; 17:14-18; 18:18-23; 20:7-18) and the imprecatory psalms (Pss. 7; 35; 69; 109; 137). Jeremiah and the psalmists also experienced great anger and bitterness (see Bowes 2018, 92-93, 368-69). Thankfully, God accepted them just as they were, even though their language got pretty ugly at times. (For further comments on this topic, → the conclusion to the sermon below, "A Violent God," p. 98.)

3. Dealing with Bitterness and Depression

Chapter 3 is very depressing when taken by itself, but there are several ways this chapter can instruct us and lead toward the healing of people's emotions.

First, chapter 3 provides a point of identification for those who have been terribly hurt by life's events. The tendency for those with traumatic experiences is to think they are the only ones with these experiences and with the emotions that inevitably follow. But Job can be a companion on the way of life for those who suffer terribly, who cry out with pain, and who agonize over their situations. He seems to ask many of the same questions that we would like to ask of God. For this reason, he can be a real friend to those who are suffering, and the things God says to him later in the book can be understood as speaking to each person who has had similar emotional traumas.

Second, chapter 3 opens a window into the souls of people who are hurting. It reminds us that there are people all around us who desperately need a friend. They probably will not ask for help because that would seem to indicate a weakness on their part. They silently bear their grief and depression in private. Some may turn to alcohol and drugs or other addictions as an escape from difficult situations. If we all would be more sensitive to the needs of those around us, this world would be a much friendlier place to live.

Third, chapter 3 provides understanding for counselors and others in the helping professions about what they are up against in trying to help people experiencing emotional trauma. Job's anger and fears might seem irrational to some, but there were real causes of his depression and reasons for his ranting: (1) the order in his world was gone, (2) the future was uncertain, and (3) God's relationship to all of Job's troubles was unknown (for a fuller discussion of these issues in Job's life, see Bowes 2018, 90-91). He felt "hedged in" (v. 23). We might surmise that Job could have entertained thoughts of suicide as a means of escape from this world's troubles (for a discussion of suicide in the Bible, see Bowes 2018, 131). Before offering helpful steps to restoration, it is important for counselors to understand the depth of hopelessness that sometimes overwhelms those who are suffering.

II. Job 3: Job's Anguish

Fourth, chapter 3 introduces us to the subject of bitterness (v. 20). Bitterness is the attitude of a person who is sour on life. It often develops when tragedies occur or when one's expectations about happiness and success are dashed. Not everyone responds to life's troubles with bitterness, but some become especially bitter and feel that they are hedged in. Or they may feel like victims whose lives are spinning out of control. In the NT, bitterness is found in a list of vices that Christians are admonished to avoid (Eph. 4:29-32; Heb. 12:14-15). It poisons one's relationships with other people and with God, and thus it is extremely harmful to one's spiritual well-being.

One of the best examples in the OT of this attitude is Naomi, who became bitter when she lost her husband and two sons (Ruth 1:13, 20). She was left to fend for herself in a foreign land with two Moabite daughters-in-law. Like Job, she believed that God had turned his hand against her (Ruth 1:13). It was not until she moved back to Israel and crossed paths with her relative Boaz that her bitterness dissipated. The marriage of her daughter-in-law Ruth to Boaz and the birth of her grandson Obed were miraculous, joyous events that revealed God's love and care for her. Her attitude about life and about God changed completely as a result.

Job was also one who slid into a depressed, bitter state of mind due to his calamities (Job 3). His bitterness did not leave him until God spoke to him in chapters 38–41. This personal encounter enabled him to gain a new understanding of God and of himself that then led to reconciliation with God and a new life of hope and well-being (→ sermon below, "Only a Novice Trying to Correct an Expert," p. 145). The examples of Job and Naomi clearly indicate that God's help is usually needed to rid oneself of this debilitating attitude of bitterness.

The point made in the preceding paragraph is not meant to suggest that all forms of bitterness and depression can be resolved by an appearance from God. Some people experience what psychologists call clinical depression, requiring help from professional counselors. In Job's case, his depression derived not only from his circumstances but also from his failure to hear from God. Once God reappeared and reminded Job of the order he had established in the world at the time of creation, then Job could put aside his bitterness and move on to a future directed by God. God's appearance was just what he needed because it brought order and divine fellowship back into his life.

4. Injustice as a Cause of Bitterness

Sometimes, like in Job's case, feelings of bitterness develop out of experiences of unjust suffering. They are really cries for justice that are directed against others (including God) who have brought harm into a person's life. These cries for justice have echoed throughout human history (e.g., Gen. 4:10), and they are still present today. Prejudices against races, nationalities, genders, social and economic classes, and religions still produce anger and bitterness. If we would stop and really listen, we would hear many cries of anguish from those who have experienced discrimination and injustice.

It is difficult to preach about these issues because in today's world many of them have become entangled in the platforms of political parties. But congregations desire and need good guidance here. The church needs preachers who will boldly shine the light of God's love and truth on *all* the experiences of life, whether uncomfortable or not. Jesus's words in the Sermon on the Mount (Matt. 5–7) certainly encourage this type of preaching from time to time.

Possible Sermon Titles: "Will the Real Job Please Stand Up?" "Dealing with Life's Emotions," "Is There a Remedy for Bitterness?" "I Wish I Could Die Right Now," "I Wish I Had Never Been Born," "Life Sometimes Seems Like a Giant Corn Maze," "Life Just Goes On and On and On"

Life's Pathway (Job 3:23)

Every person is on a way/pathway in life. The Bible speaks of this concept frequently. So preachers and teachers have a ready-made topic that can borrow ideas from a number of other biblical passages.

In essence, a person's way/pathway is a metaphor for the sum of one's life experiences beginning with birth and ending with death. It includes not only the activities of life but also one's thoughts, attitudes, and plans. The ideas of direction and destiny are always connected with the concept of way, because a pathway goes from one place to another. People should be especially concerned about the destinations that lie at the end of the pathways on which they are traveling. One of the important responsibilities of parents is to help their children get established on the best way and encourage them to continue on it after they leave home (Prov. 22:6).

The Bible makes use of this pathway imagery to encourage people to walk on a way that is pleasing to God. In fact, it narrows the number of

II. Job 3: Job's Anguish

spiritual pathways to only two—the way of the righteous and the way of the wicked. No middle road exists. According to Psalm 1, each of these two ways has its own lifestyle and destiny. People are encouraged to choose God's way, which is "the way of the righteous," because "the way of the wicked leads to destruction" (v. 6). Disobedience leads to God's judgment. In Deuteronomy 10:12-13, Moses encouraged Israel "to fear the Lord your God, to walk in obedience to him, to love him, to serve the Lord your God with all your heart and with all your soul, and to observe the Lord's commands and decrees that I am giving you today for your own good." In the book of Proverbs, the way of the righteous is connected with "wisdom" and "knowledge" (1:7), while the way of the wicked is exemplified in the life of the fool, the simpleminded, and the scoffer.

The concept of the two spiritual ways is found repeatedly in the Wisdom Literature, the Psalms, and the Prophets, so it is no surprise that Jesus incorporated this concept into his teachings. A few examples are the narrow way versus the broad way (Matt. 7:13-14), the wise virgins/bridesmaids versus the foolish virgins/bridesmaids (25:1-13), and the man who built his house on the rock versus the man who built his house on the sand (7:24-27).

However, even as important as one's way in life is, there are times when one cannot find the correct pathway. The way becomes hidden from view. People feel lost and unsure of the next step to take. This can happen for a variety of reasons.

Sometimes people make bad choices that lead them into a dead end. There is simply no way forward. At other times the actions of other people cause roadblocks that have to be cleared before one can proceed. Even natural disasters can cover one's pathway with floods or shroud it in such thick fog that one cannot see which way to go.

In Job 3:23, Job is speaking of a different kind of obstruction to his pathway—one caused by God. For some unknown reason, God has hedged Job in, in what feels like a giant corn maze or labyrinth. He cannot see ahead, behind, around, over, or under the obstructions that God has placed around him. His journey through life has come to a standstill that cannot proceed until God removes the obstructions and/or explains why they happened.

Here is a good place to discuss the causes of suffering (the obstructions of life) presented in the book of Job. There are several: punishment for sin; divine discipline; the Examiner's test of a person's faith; the

II. Job 3: Job's Anguish

actions of other people; natural disasters; the imperfect, sinful nature of humanity that originated in the garden of Eden; and so forth (for a fuller discussion, see Bowes 2018, 408-9, as well as the sermon below, "The Nature of Suffering," p. 159).

This discussion will enlarge people's understanding of the variety of obstructions that may block the view of one's pathway. Only one cause seems to be related to bad moral choices. Most of the others are out of our control and thus not preventable. Therefore, obstructions (including all types of suffering) are life experiences that most of us can expect at some time in our lives.

What is somewhat discouraging about all of this is that the specific reason for our suffering is often a mystery. We may not know the exact cause. For this reason, we can identify with Job's frustration and anguish in chapter 3 in not knowing what he needed to do to address the cause.

So what is the best course of action to take when one's way is obstructed? Here is where Job provides some guidance for those whose lives have gone topsy-turvy (42:1-6; see Bowes 2018, 393-97). Job never received a satisfactory explanation of the obstructions in his life, but yet he was able to continue a meaningful existence for many more decades. How did he do this? He survived through "submission to God, obedience to his will, trust in his wisdom, and acceptance of life's mysteries that come our way" (Bowes 2018, 413; → also sermon above, "When Life Goes Topsy-Turvy," p. 31).

Chapter 3 raises an additional question: If God is the cause of Job's suffering (through his use of his Examiner), what does this imply about the nature of God? How could a good and loving God bring such terrible pain into the life of the saint of whom he is most proud? And what does this imply about God's desire for justice in this world?

This is an additional topic that could be touched on briefly here or developed later (→ "Conclusion: Major Theological Themes" below, p. 157). In any case, this topic needs to be addressed somewhere in a series of sermons from Job because it is a prominent question in the minds of many people.

Possible Sermon Titles: "The Two Ways," "Way to Go!" "When There's No Visible Pathway Ahead," "Obstructions along the Way of Life"

III. JOB 4–27: THE THREE FRIENDS

The dialogue section of Job (chs. 4–27) is difficult to organize into units for preaching. It is long as well as repetitious, and the speakers keep changing every few chapters. For that reason, why not consider a different approach? Instead of preaching chronologically through the chapters, try grouping together all of the chapters for each speaker and present at least one sermon on each one. This gives you the opportunity to develop the whole character of each speaker while commenting on their arguments. Separate sermons on Eliphaz (chs. 4–5, 15, 22), Bildad (chs. 8, 18, 25; 24:18-24), and Zophar (chs. 11, 20; 27:13-23) would be appropriate, followed by several on Job's responses (chs. 6–7, 9–10, 12–14, 16–17, 19, 21, 23–24, 26–27).

You probably should begin this section with some general statements to inform the congregation about the nature of the dialogues. There are several principles to keep in mind.

First, the speeches in this section are not a normal human dialogue. They are more like a series of debating points that the author has created to present different sides of an argument concerning the cause of Job's suffering and what he needs to do to find relief. Each of the friends speaks in the same order through three cycles, and each of their speeches receives an immediate response from Job. Sometimes there are personal attacks that get pretty heated, but no one ever interrupts another speaker or gets out of order.

Second, one should refrain from classifying the characters as either good or bad. Each character is doing his best to solve the mystery of Job's suffering without any knowledge of the divine conversation in the prologue between God and the Examiner. The fact that they are missing crucial pieces of evidence results in the misdiagnosis of the real reason for Job's troubles. They attribute it to divine punishment even though it has nothing to do with punishment. This should be a warning to us about the dangers of prejudging others without knowing all the evidence. Even though our logic may be excellent, as it was with the friends, faulty premises will undermine our arguments and conclusions.

Third, each speech has a context that needs to be preserved. One cannot just quote one verse and assume that it is true or false based on the speaker. The entire book is needed to make a proper evaluation of the participants and their views. And certainly, God's speeches at the end (chs. 38–41) are necessary to provide a context for all the speeches in the dialogues.

Fourth, everything the friends present is part of what biblical scholars call the wisdom theology. This theology had ancient roots that went back to some of the earliest human writings. It was picked up by the wisdom writers in the OT. It was supported by the prophets. It was re-emphasized in many of Jesus's teachings. And it is still believed by many people today. But is this the whole answer to the problem of suffering? Again, we need to look at the entire book to answer that question.

Basically, the wisdom theology supports the concept that all people receive the exact amount of reward or punishment that corresponds to the choices they make in life. There are no exceptions. Justice always prevails. Consequently, it is important to know and follow the rules of life that God has established in order to live a successful life.

Some readers of the book are going to like what the three friends say. But does the wisdom theology provide a good answer to *all* of life's troubles? And how does the wisdom theology relate to what God says in chapters 38–41? Are the two in agreement? Here one should make a careful analysis, for the answer is more complicated than a simple yes or no. This will be dealt with later.

The best approach to the dialogues is to listen carefully to what each character is saying and how the other speakers are reacting. Is each person telling the whole truth or just the part he wants to emphasize? Is there good evidence to support their conclusions? Job needs to be evaluated in the same way. He is supposed to be the hero in the book, but he is strongly criticized by God at the very end. So his speeches need the same kind of critical analysis as those of the three friends.

III. Job 4–27: The Three Friends

Eliphaz (Job 4–5, 15, 22)

1. Suffering Is Inevitable (Job 4–5)

The first thing one notices about Eliphaz's first speech is its gentleness. In later parts of the book the atmosphere will get nasty as Bildad and Zophar enter the dialogues, but Eliphaz begins with great tact and kindness. He is an older gentleman who senses that Job is in need of a friend and some encouragement. It is true that Eliphaz was as shocked as the other two friends by Job's appearance and his emotional ranting in chapter 3, but he was not put off by Job's bluster. He felt an urgent need to respond as soon as Job was finished speaking.

There are two important points that Eliphaz wished to bring to Job's attention in this speech. The first was the inevitability of suffering for all human beings. No one can avoid it. And the second was a plan of action to deal with suffering. What could Job do to relieve it?

a. Suffering Is Inevitable

No one likes to suffer, but the truth is that we cannot avoid it for three reasons. First, suffering is inevitable because we are sinful from birth (5:6-7). We are finite human creatures with a proneness to sin. As Eliphaz says, we are "born to trouble, as surely as sparks fly upward" (v. 7). There is some question about how to translate the word for "sparks," but the concept is clear. Our troubles in life do not come from the environment or others. They are caused by us. They are the consequences of our sinful human nature. We are morally flawed and thus prone to get ourselves into trouble. This thought has obvious connections with the story of the fall in Genesis 3. But the book of Job is not concerned with how this human condition developed, only that it is now present and affects every human being. Because Job participated in the human condition, he could not avoid the suffering that was caused by it.

Second, suffering is inevitable because human beings are so inferior to God (Job 4:17). The translation of 4:17 should read something like the following: "Can any human being [claim to] be righteous in the presence of God? Can any man [claim to] be pure in the presence of his Creator?" (AT). This is especially evident in the area of morality (vv. 17-18), but it is also true with regard to the security of our dwelling (v. 19), our time (v. 20), and our wisdom (v. 21). There is truly a "Grand Canyon" between us and God. The implication is that if humans were holier, like

God, they could eliminate suffering from their lives. But alas, God's level of purity is unattainable.

This concept came to Eliphaz by means of a vision in the night (vv. 12-17). A spooky shape, which he assumed to be divine, appeared before him one night. It told him that there was a tremendous moral gulf between God and humanity. In fact, God is so pure and holy that even the angels seem corrupt. How much more corrupt are human beings, who are farther removed from God?

If desired, you can spend some time here discussing the transcendence of God (see Bowes 2018, 109-10). What does that mean for humanity? Is the gap between us so great that even communication with God is unlikely? Is it ever possible for humans to cross this great divide and enter the presence of God? Or are we forever doomed to remain in our sinful separation from almighty God because he is so holy?

In answer to these questions, Job will wish later in the book for an intermediary or mediator to bridge the gap between himself and God (9:33-35; 16:19; 19:25-27). Someone such as an angel might fulfill that role for Job. But Eliphaz anticipated that possibility by pointing out that even the angels could not perform the task of an intermediary. So there was no use in calling on them (5:1; reemphasized in 15:15-16 and by Bildad in 25:4-6). Deep in his heart Job knew there was no such person.

You might follow up this gloomy scenario with a few comments on the NT approach to transcendence. Christ, the God-human, bridged the gap and became the intermediary that Job desperately needed and wanted. He did this, not in the way that Job hoped for (by explaining the cause of his suffering), but in a totally new and unique way that cost him his life but provided salvation for all. By putting the two Testaments together, there really is a great gulf between the divine and the human, between the infinite and the finite. We humans are in a terrible predicament. But God in his great mercy provided the necessary means to draw us together, thus opening the door to fellowship and salvation.

Third, suffering is inevitable because everyone is in need of discipline from time to time (5:17-27). There are areas of our lives that need to be improved. Even a supersaint like Job was not perfect. Just like a good parent, God sees when we have become too careless or too self-centered or too apathetic. He sees a need for a good spanking or a session in time-out. His discipline may be considered unpleasant, and he knows we will suffer.

But he does it with a purpose in mind. Correction and transformation are his goals, not destruction (see Bowes 2018, 120-21).

The good news is that God's discipline is only temporary. Once the discipline has resulted in changed behavior, then God removes the suffering and restores and heals. A person who has been disciplined will be a better person in the long run and will come to the end of his or her days with the full satisfaction of a life well lived. Eliphaz believed that Job could be experiencing God's discipline.

If this is the case, one should react to God's discipline with joy, for it means that God cares about us (5:17). He is trying to improve us. This is the hope that Eliphaz offered to Job.

The point Eliphaz was trying to make is that no one can completely avoid the troubles of life. Good choices may spare us some measure of suffering. For example, quitting smoking has been proven to better one's health. But one good choice such as avoiding smoking does not spare us from all illnesses in life. In the NT, Jesus confirmed Eliphaz's point that people should not be surprised when trouble comes their way: "In this world you will have trouble" (John 16:33). Suffering is inevitable.

b. Eliphaz Suggested Three Things That Job Could Do to Relieve His Suffering and/or to Shorten Its Duration

First, follow your own advice. Practice what you used to preach to others (4:6). Eliphaz knew that Job used to support many people in his community who were suffering (vv. 3-4). He was always there to help when someone had a need. Eliphaz's comments on this are very brief, but you can add from Job's own words in 29:11-17.

In Eliphaz's mind, the kind of compassion that Job engaged in deserved mention because it illustrated Job's basic integrity and righteousness. He did not just talk about helping other people. He gave of his means and lifted up the downtrodden. He truly deserved the "Good Citizen of the Year" award from the people of Uz.

But now the roles were reversed. Job had lost the means to help others. He was suffering and in need of someone to stand by him as a friend. Eliphaz's evaluation was that Job had gotten a little off track in his thinking because of his tremendous losses. He just needed someone to point him back to the main pathway, and then he could go on living as he always had. Eliphaz's message to Job was basically this: "Follow the advice that you used to give to others who were suffering. It will help you get through your own troubles. And someday God will reward you again just as he used to."

To encourage Job to forget his present troubles and reclaim his former integrity, Eliphaz reminded Job of two principles that had undergirded his life in prior years: (1) his solid faith in God ("piety") and (2) his "blameless" character (4:6). Job certainly agreed that these practices had been important to him in former days, for he mentions them several times in his later speeches and then summarizes how God had blessed him (ch. 29).

Second, trust in God's just ways in dealing with the world (4:7-9). Eliphaz believed that God never harms or allows harm to come to an innocent person. The righteous are always rewarded, and the wicked are always punished. It is a universal principle that all people receive exactly what they deserve in life.

We will see in Job's later speeches that he disagreed extremely with this point. Job was a supersaint, as holy as a righteous person could be, and yet he still had suffered tremendous losses that were caused by God. Therefore, Eliphaz's principle that all people reap what they sow was not true when applied to Job. Righteous people like Job sometimes do have their goods stolen by marauding bandits. Righteous parents sometimes do lose their children to a mighty windstorm. And perfectly healthy, righteous people sometimes are afflicted with painful diseases that lead toward an early death. It is also true that bad people sometimes are never punished for their wickedness.

The way that Eliphaz arrived at his belief in the absolute justice of God was through cause-and-effect reasoning. Somewhere in a series of sermons from Job, preachers need to speak about this method of reasoning, for it can result in serious misinterpretations of biblical passages. All three friends were guilty of this error in reasoning, so the topic can be addressed in several places. This is one of them (for a discussion of the issue and its ramifications, see "Cause-and-Effect Reasoning" in Bowes 2018, 101-3).

Eliphaz knew that sin causes suffering. He also knew that Job was now suffering in the extreme. Therefore, working backward from the effect to the cause, he believed that Job must have sinned and must be experiencing the punishment for that sin. The problem with this line of reasoning could be illustrated to your congregation by choosing several verses in Proverbs and discussing right and wrong interpretations

III. Job 4-27: The Three Friends

of them using cause-and-effect reasoning. The one on raising children (Prov. 22:6) is especially appropriate because many parents with broken hearts have questioned pastors about its application to their own family setting. Proverbs 22:6 is a good principle overall, but it does not allow for exceptions to the rule caused by such things as human free will and the influences of other people outside the family.

Third, seek God above all else (Job 5:8). This word of advice lies at the heart of the Wisdom Literature. Seeking God is always the right way to live no matter what our circumstances because God is so awesome in power and wisdom. The "wonders" and "miracles" listed in 5:9-16 are only a small sampling of the types of things that God is capable of doing. Even the poorest and neediest of human beings can experience hope for the future if they seek this mighty God (vv. 15-16). The irony of this point is that Job had been doing exactly that for many decades, and yet he still suffered horrendous losses.

In evaluating Eliphaz's overall advice to Job, we must give him credit for pointing out the inevitability of suffering. Trouble will eventually come to all of us. However, his recommendations concerning how to deal with suffering were not helpful at all because he was ignorant of the real reason for Job's troubles. That should make us think twice before offering easy solutions to people who are deeply troubled.

One way to conclude the sermon would be to challenge people to think about what they would say to another person who had lost a loved one. What words are appropriate, biblical, and comforting in those situations? Should we say the kinds of things that Eliphaz said to Job? Too many well-intentioned people say the wrong things to people who are grieving. Eliphaz's speech to Job contained a few helpful ways of looking at suffering, but overall it was certainly not the right thing to say to someone who had just lost ten children.

Goldingay suggests that before we attempt to counsel someone who is suffering or grieving, we need to consider two thoughts (2013, 83-84). First, do we really need to say anything at all? Silence and hugs and tears are often more effective than words in conveying our concern. And second, there really isn't much to say anyway, other than "I love you and I'm praying for you." Most often, people's presence is needed and appreciated much more than their words.

Possible Sermon Titles: "Do People Always Reap What They Sow?" "An Agricultural Explanation of Suffering," "Cause and Effect: Is It Valid in

III. Job 4–27: The Three Friends

Explaining Life's Troubles?" "Appropriate Words for People Who Are Suffering," "Who Can Bridge the Gap?" "We Are Made of Lesser Stuff," "When God Sends Us to Time-Out"

2. How Do You Know What You Know? (Job 4–5)

One of the issues that faces the reader of the book of Job is the problem of sorting out truth from falsehood. All the speakers seem convinced that truth is on their side. They are very passionate about the logical consistency of their arguments and the correctness of their views. Who is to be believed when major differences of opinion arise between speakers?

Newsom suggests that we should think about this issue from the standpoint of "religious epistemology"—how do we know what we know? (1996, 453). What sources of information, what authorities, do we draw upon to establish and support our belief systems? While the book does not discuss this topic directly, it does reveal the ways that each of the characters formed his belief system. Eliphaz's speeches appealed to three sources of truth that he believed supported his views.

First, he appealed to an "external (i.e., non-human) authority" (Newsom 1996, 453). His use of a divine visitation is a good example of this approach (4:12-21). A direct word from one's deity (i.e., "God said to me") is a trump card that is almost impossible to challenge. His use of nature is another example of a nonhuman authority (vv. 10-11; 15:33). The natural world provides analogies that can be applied to human behavior along parallel lines.

Second, Eliphaz relied heavily on tradition—the "authority of consensus" (Newsom 1996, 453). A person usually adopts the belief system of the community of which the person is a part. In the case of Eliphaz, he had adopted the beliefs of the wisdom theology that stretched back for hundreds of years (5:27; 15:10, 18). If the sages before him had believed this way and proven its truthfulness, then it must be true.

Across America today, there are communities that have a decidedly conservative view of life, and there are others that support a more progressive approach. The people living in these communities generally have the impression that their belief system is the correct one because everyone in their neighborhood believes the same way. Eliphaz's belief system was based on an authority of consensus that derived from the beliefs of hundreds of people. Only in his case, these people were not related to

III. Job 4–27: The Three Friends

him geographically. They were the hundreds of wisdom thinkers (sages) who had lived before him.

Third, Eliphaz appealed to his own "individual experience" (Newsom 1996, 453). People's experiences in life usually contribute to the formation of their belief system. We all learn a great deal in the school of hard knocks. Eliphaz mentions three times how this happened to him (4:8; 5:3; 15:17). The problem with placing too much emphasis on this particular approach is that everyone's experiences are different.

Each of Eliphaz's three sources of information is valid up to a certain point. They may rightly contribute some support to a person's way of thinking. And we all have probably appealed to all three in some of our discussions with others. But a good belief system must be worked out in community because everyone has blind spots that must be called out by others in the community. All voices in a community have a right to be heard, even if they are based on weak or faulty evidence, but not every view is a good one. Some views are based on authorities that are naive, biased, or just plain wrong. They need to be identified for what they are.

Over the centuries the church has appealed to several authorities that were not mentioned by Eliphaz: the actions and teachings of Jesus, biblical examples that illustrate God's approval or disapproval of specific behaviors or attitudes, and theological positions that the church has developed over centuries of time such as the Apostles' Creed. Individuals can assume that they are on good ground when their personal positions are supported by a variety of good sources. Nevertheless, a humble attitude is always proper when seeking the truth.

One possible conclusion to this sermon could be an attempt to help a congregation develop ways of speaking tolerantly about the views of others. Job and his three friends were sometimes very disrespectful of each other. Zophar's pointed jab at Job in 11:12 is probably the best example of how quickly conversations can turn ugly. Intolerance, words of insult and ridicule, and demonizing have no place in the body of Christ. We are called to be peacemakers (Matt. 5:9).

Effective peacemaking requires lots of serious communication. It means taking the time to listen to opposing points of view. Toleration of another person's viewpoint does not necessarily mean agreement, but it does open the door to communication. It is amazing how much we learn from others when we really listen without judgment.

It is appropriate when speaking with other persons about their viewpoints to ask them to identify the sources of their information. Where have they found evidence to support their conclusions? Often this practice provides insight into why people hold certain views. For example, were their political views formed from listening to CNN or Fox News? Were their theological views and religious practices formed from growing up in a Protestant church or the Roman Catholic Church?

Peacemaking also requires us to respect each person in a community as one of God's children. None of us are superior to others when we stand before God. And finally, peacemaking demands that we be willing to work in community with others to arrive at a position that takes all views seriously and develops a solution that is the best for the group as a whole.

Possible Sermon Titles: "Sources Matter," "The Truth, the Whole Truth, and Nothing but the Truth," "'Tolerance' Is Not a Bad Word," "Peacemaking: A Godly Practice"

3. The Wicked Live Terrible Lives (Job 15)

When people get angry in an argument, they sometimes discard their logical train of thought and stoop to personal attacks against their opponent's character. They also tend to repeat earlier arguments but at a higher volume. Such was the case with Eliphaz in his second speech.

In his first speech, Eliphaz had complimented Job on his earlier righteous life and gently tried to instruct him in some of the basic principles of the wisdom theology. The primary one was the belief that God always rewards the righteous and punishes the wicked. We reap what we sow.

By the second speech, Eliphaz had heard Job speak three more times. He was becoming alarmed at Job's lack of knowledge, even though he claimed to have great wisdom. And he was very upset that Job refused to accept the advice of the three friends. In fact, Job had even accused the friends of being deceitful. Eliphaz wanted to know how Job could claim to be wise and yet speak like a fool. Job sounded more like a sinner than a sage. He talked as if he were the only wise person in the world, but his words were nothing more than hot air. Further, he was undermining other people's faith in God.

Job 15:10 could be interpreted in one of two ways. Eliphaz could be claiming that the ancient wisdom theology was on his side. It supported the beliefs of the friends. Eliphaz certainly believed that. However, it

III. Job 4-27: The Three Friends

could also be a claim for superior knowledge based on Eliphaz's greater age than Job. In either case, Eliphaz refused to credit Job with any wisdom at all. Both the ancient sages and the friends were on the side of truth, whereas Job was totally ignorant. Eliphaz also repeated his earlier comment from his first speech that all human beings are inferior to God and sinful by nature. Apparently, he was disturbed that Job refused to believe that he was now a sinner.

The remainder of Eliphaz's second speech (15:17-35) is a description of the terrible life that wicked people must endure. Some people think that God's punishment of the wicked occurs mainly after death but that during this life they enjoy untold pleasures and success. Eliphaz and the wisdom theology believed differently. For them, the life of the wicked is literally a hell on earth. (1) The wicked experience emotional turmoil and terror every day (v. 20). (2) They are attacked by evil plunderers who rob them of their goods (v. 21). (3) They cannot find their way in life because they are surrounded by darkness (v. 22). (4) They have to scavenge for their food (v. 23). (5) They lose their wealth and are forced to live in ruined towns (v. 29). (6) Their homes and families are destroyed (v. 34). (7) And they die at an early age (v. 32). Eliphaz's points here need further expansion, maybe with some biblical examples of what happened to some of Israel's wicked kings.

What does this have to do with Job? Eliphaz believed that Job needed to be warned about the consequences of sin before it was too late. Job was headed toward the life of a sinner, if he was not there already. This speech was intended as a wake-up call. Why would anyone choose the life of a sinner knowing that it produced terrible consequences in this life?

But even more subtly, Eliphaz was hinting that Job might already be experiencing God's judgment. Even though Job denied being a sinner, he had admitted that he was enduring many of the same consequences that sinners experience. For example, Job had acknowledged that he was terrified of God (7:14; 9:34; 13:21). Eliphaz was quick to point out that wicked people also were terrified of God (15:24). Thus there was a strong possibility that Job might already be experiencing God's punishment for his sin. For Eliphaz, "Job looked like a sinner, talked like a sinner, acted like a sinner, and was being punished like a sinner. Therefore he must be one" (Bowes 2018, 210).

The remainder of this sermon could focus on appropriate passages from the Gospels and the Pauline Epistles that deal with the wages of sin. According to the NT, what are the wages of sin in this life? Do the wages of sin affect other people or just oneself? Do people know if they are experiencing the wages of sin? And how do the wages of sin affect life after death?

The conclusion to this sermon could describe the remedy for sin and its wages. What is God's plan of salvation that he now offers through Christ? And how can we access this hope for ourselves? Romans 1–8 is a good resource for this section of the sermon.

One additional way to approach Job 15 is as follows. Eliphaz, Bildad, and Zophar all offered hope to Job in their first speeches (chs. 4–5, 8, 11). But by the time of their second speeches (chs. 15, 18, 20), they had become considerably agitated at Job's stubbornness. Their purpose in these second speeches was principally to point out the terrible life that befell wicked people. They hoped that their description of the wages of sin would somehow convince Job to confess his own sins and thus be restored into God's favor.

With that in mind, you may wish to combine all of the second speeches (chs. 15, 18, 20) into one sermon that focuses on the theology of sin. I attempt to do a little of this at the end of Zophar's second speech (→ sermon below, "God's Sudden Reversals," p. 79). But there is much more to preach on if the views of all three friends are combined.

Possible Sermon Titles: "The Wages of Sin," "God's Remedy for Sin," "Reconciliation with God Is Possible Now"

4. Repent of Your Wickedness! (Job 22)

In his third speech, Eliphaz finally unloads on Job, accusing him of great "wickedness" (22:5). He follows this accusation with a list of the sins that he believes Job may have committed. These mostly concern the kinds of sins that a rich, powerful person might inflict on the poor and needy.

However, he offers no proof that Job had done these things. And further, his words are actually a contradiction of his praise for Job back in his first speech (4:3-4). Apparently, Eliphaz had finally reached his emotional limit. Job's repeated denials of sin and his attacks against the friends had left Eliphaz exhausted. In desperation he lashes out with the first direct charge of sin against Job in the book, although he cannot prove it. In previous speeches, all three friends had hinted that Job

III. Job 4-27: The Three Friends

might be a sinner. But this speech is the first face-to-face accusation of sin that the friends have hurled at Job.

Eliphaz follows up his accusation with an attack against something Job said in his last speech. In 21:22 Job had stated that God did not know how to judge people correctly. The fact that righteous people suffered calamities while wicked people lived successful lives was proof that God needed someone to instruct him about the principles of justice. Eliphaz's reaction to this statement by Job was that God knew full well what he was doing. He saw every sinner and every righteous person, and he always judged each correctly. In Eliphaz's mind, Job's complaint was a typical response from someone who felt he had suffered unjustly. It was easier to blame someone else, in this case God, than to accept one's own responsibility.

Eliphaz's final words to Job are a call to repentance. If Job would just follow Eliphaz's advice and agree with God concerning his sin, then God would restore him back to prosperity and health. God and Job would be reconciled, and Job would once again "delight" in the Lord (22:26).

It is amazing that one of the friends still believes that Job has a bright future ahead of him. Even after all of Job's losses, even after his stubborn attitude toward the friends, even after his supposed hypocritical denial of sin, and even after his rebellion against God, Eliphaz still believed that Job could change. And if Job would change, God would change also.

Although Eliphaz was wrong about a lot of things over the course of the dialogues, he was entirely correct about this final point. For this is the essence of the gospel. It is good news. We all have the capacity and the opportunity to change from our sinful ways. And if we will do so, God will change his attitude toward us as well and welcome us back into fellowship with him. God is the "Hound of Heaven,"* seeking out all human beings and offering them a new life. Eliphaz's offer of hope to Job is exactly what God provides for each individual.

Unfortunately, Eliphaz had completely misunderstood Job's situation and thus had offered him the wrong remedy. But the remedy was and

---

*See Francis Thompson, "The Hound of Heaven," in *The Oxford Book of English Mystical Verse*, ed. D. H. S. Nicholson and A. H. E. Lee (Oxford, UK: Clarendon, 1917), 409-15, https://archive.org/details/oxfordbookofengl00nichuoft/page/408/mode/2up.

still is a good one for those who are sinners. "Agree with God," he says, "and return to him." And when we do, our lives are changed.

So how should we evaluate Eliphaz? He was an older man with a genuine desire to help. He offered Job the best advice he could, based on his knowledge of the wisdom theology. His statements arguing for the inevitability of suffering were generally correct. Every one of us is going to suffer in life. And his words of encouragement for Job to practice what he had preached to others and to seek God were sound advice. Seeking God should be the number one priority in everyone's life.

However, Eliphaz was wrong in assuming that Job was being punished. He fell into the trap of prejudging people based on appearance and deduced that Job must have committed a terrible sin. We know from the prologue that Job was not being punished at all. He was being tested for the quality of his faith. Eliphaz was also wrong in believing that justice always prevails in this world. Some very unjust things happen on a regular basis, and God does not always intervene. This creates a lot of problems for us in explaining God's relationship to the world. But that is a topic for another day.

Eliphaz's most important words are his offer of hope to Job. Job's future can be better than the present. Everyone in the world needs to hear that message, for we can become so discouraged about our world, even when we are not suffering. As Christians, we trace that hope to Jesus Christ. Eliphaz bases it on something else just as important. He bases it on the awesomeness of God who "performs wonders that cannot be fathomed, miracles that cannot be counted" (5:9). If we will reject wickedness (22:23) and accept this God and his instructions to us (vv. 21-22), we will be reconciled to God. This is the hope that Eliphaz offered to Job and that God still offers to every human being.

Possible Sermon Titles: "Agree with God," "The Consequences of Sin Are Real," "Real Hope for All"

Bildad (Job 8, 18, 25)

1. God Does Not Pervert Justice (Job 8)

Bildad, the second of the three friends to speak, was a much different personality than Eliphaz. His primary focus was on the great wisdom

III. Job 4-27: The Three Friends

principles of the past that had guided civilization for centuries. For this reason, he is often called the traditionalist.

By the time Bildad enters the dialogues, he had already heard Job speak twice. Both times upset him. Job had claimed in his first speech that he was so miserable that he longed to die. In his second speech, Job had stated that his death was imminent. He wished that God would leave him alone so he could die in peace. Job believed that God was continually attacking him both day and night. He was terrified of God and wanted to exit this life into Sheol (the place of the dead) as quickly as possible. From Bildad's viewpoint, Job did not sound like a righteous person. How could an individual be so discouraged with life that he wished to die?

Further, Job had accused God of attacking him unjustly. Bildad saw that as impossible and jumped to God's defense. "How can you say that, Job? God has never 'pervert[ed] justice' [8:3]. Your belief is heresy. Don't you know that God is a *just* God by definition?"

To make his point, Bildad used the death of Job's children as an illustration (v. 4). "Job, your children had to have died for a reason. This tragedy did not happen by accident. Your children may have sinned against God, and he simply imposed on them the consequences of their sins. God would have been completely just to do this."

This was a terribly insensitive and cruel remark by Bildad that no doubt tore at Job's heart. Bildad had no tact. He had obviously never taken a course in counseling. One should never blame another person's children for causing their own suffering, for in a very subtle way, it is accusing the parents of not raising their children right. But Bildad did not recognize this at all. No doubt, he would say in his own defense that the first word of verse 4 is "if" (not "when" [NIV]): "If your children sinned . . ." It was only a possibility, not a direct accusation. But Job knew exactly what Bildad was implying, for this principle lay at the heart of the wisdom theology. Sin always results in suffering. Therefore, the death of Job's children must have been caused by their sins.

Bildad had a strong belief that people who turn away from God are creating for themselves a life devoid of "hope," "confidence," and "trust" (vv. 13-14, NASB). Their lives may appear to flourish for a season, but sooner or later they will experience God's judgment and die an early death. Even their very existence will be forgotten by those who remain.

III. Job 4-27: The Three Friends

To illustrate his point, Bildad presents three examples of situations in nature that show the fleeting, unstable life of the "godless" (v. 13). The first is the "papyrus" plant that grows to a great height along the edges of rivers and lakes (vv. 11-13). But as soon as the water recedes, the papyrus quickly withers away. Without water, the plants are doomed. Similarly, without God, people are doomed.

The second illustration concerns the fragility of "a spider's web" (vv. 14-15). The intricate beauty of a web is stunning, but it is not designed to withstand heavy pressure. One who leans against it for support will find that it quickly "gives way." Similarly, those who put their trust in things other than God soon find that those things collapse in short order.

Bildad returns to another type of flourishing "plant" for his third illustration (vv. 16-19). This plant grows like a vine, sending its runners along the ground and over the rocks. Nothing seems to stop it. But apparently this plant is considered a weed by the farmer, for at some point in its life, it is pulled up and thrown away. Its existence is ended and forgotten. The implication is that God deals the same kind of blow to the godless as the farmer imposes on the vine.

In all three illustrations, the point is that life without God is hopeless, unstable, and fleeting. The wicked experience an early death.

So where is hope to be found in this life? Bildad returns to the main principle of the wisdom theology that Eliphaz mentioned earlier (5:8). "Seek God earnestly." Even "plead with the Almighty" (8:5). This last verb is used in many psalms where the author is pleading for God to show mercy.

Bildad finds support for his advice from two sources. The first is his confidence that God always accepts those who turn to him (v. 20). He never rejects those who seek him with their whole heart. He welcomes them and fills their lives with "joy" and "laughter" (v. 21).

The second reason Bildad believes he speaks the truth is his confidence in the trustworthiness of the wisdom traditions (vv. 8-10). Former generations had taught him that those who seek God are always blessed and rewarded in this life. There are no exceptions to this rule. How can one not rely on a principle that has been proven true over and over again across many centuries of time?

The most positive words that Bildad offers to Job focus on a better life in the future. "Job, you may feel that God is punishing you now. But you will have a much better future if you seek out God instead of criticizing him and whining. God is just, and 'he will rouse himself on your behalf and restore you to your prosperous state' [v. 6]. Doesn't that get you excited?"

The law of retribution is the main topic of all of Bildad's speeches. He strongly believed that in this life God always acts in positive ways toward the righteous and in negative ways toward the wicked (v. 20; 18:5-21). This is a hard-and-fast principle that God enforces throughout his moral universe. It is supported by many parts of the OT, such as the book of Proverbs and the Prophets. And it was taught by many wisdom thinkers in other cultures stretching back to the earliest human writers.

The law of retribution also receives lip service from many people today. Here is a place where you can provide some contemporary examples (e.g., the attack on the World Trade Center in 2001) to show that some people still use the law of retribution to interpret life's tragedies (see Bowes 2018, 158-59). In their minds, every flood, fire, hurricane, tornado, and earthquake is a punishment from God against someone's sin. But they are never able to provide proof that God intended these disasters in that way. And they have no way of explaining why good Christian people are also harmed by these disasters, if God intended them as retribution. Unfortunately and sadly, these people do great harm to God's kingdom by casting God as a powerful, frightening tyrant and by always blaming the victims of suffering for causing their own troubles.

The law of retribution is a powerful, straightforward, and simple message about judgment on the wicked and hope for the righteous. It has been around for a long time, so how can we fault Bildad for speaking to Job in this way? After all, as the traditionalist, he was bringing the experiences of thousands of people to Job's (and our) attention. Where did he go wrong?

Bildad's reliance on the law of retribution can be faulted for three reasons. First, he did not have all the evidence needed to make a good evaluation of Job's situation. He had no knowledge of the heavenly conversation described in the prologue. He just assumed that Job's suffering had something to do with sin. And therefore if sin was at the root of the problem, Job needed to "seek God" (8:5). He needed to become "pure and upright" (v. 6) before God would bless him again. But Bildad's diagnosis missed the mark because Job was already pure and upright (1:1). For this reason, his remedy for Job's troubles was flawed as well.

Second, in addition to misdiagnosing Job's condition, Bildad was mistaken about the consequences of sin. His belief that all wicked people have short life spans as a result of their sins (8:11-13; 18:5-6; 24:18-24) was without any proof. Many may die early as a result of bringing harm to their physical bodies, but some live long lives, as Job observed (21:7-34).

Those today who make authoritative pronouncements about the relationship between sin and natural disasters make the same mistake. They have no evidence whatsoever that sin has caused such tragedies. Yet they act as if they know the mind of God on these matters. But we, the readers, know that Bildad was completely wrong. It is true that sin can cause suffering, but we know from the prologue that Job's suffering had nothing to do with sin. It was a test of the motivation for his righteousness. Further, we know that suffering can occur for many reasons other than sin. And Eliphaz already noted one of these in his first speech—for divine discipline (5:17-27). Apparently Bildad was not listening too closely to his friend Eliphaz.

Third, Bildad assumed that God always acts in observable and direct ways without exceptions, paradoxes, or mystery. His governance of the world is always predictable, dependable, and understandable by human beings. But the OT does not support such a hypothesis. In Job's case, Job was an obvious exception to the law of retribution. He was totally righteous according to the prologue, and yet he suffered. And many other OT heroes of the faith endured similar troubles, such as Abraham and Moses. The wisdom theology did not know how to diagnose a person who was both righteous and experiencing suffering. Its proponents had no category for such an individual because they did not believe in unjust suffering. This was an impossibility because it implied that God was unjust. Therefore Bildad, as well as the other friends, based their evaluation of Job's situation on a faulty understanding of God.

The book of Job teaches us that human suffering can occur for many reasons (see "The Nature of Suffering" in Bowes 2018, 408-9). And everyday life teaches us that suffering comes to everyone, whether we are righteous or sinful. So the use of the law of retribution to explain all of life's troubles is totally wrong, and people who use it in that way are misguided.

Let's return to Bildad's original rhetorical question: "Does God pervert justice?" (8:3). If Job is correct that God allows righteous people like himself to suffer and wicked people to avoid punishment, can we still claim that God is just? This is a difficult topic that has received much comment from theologians across the centuries. Here is the book of Job's contribution to the debate (found primarily in God's speeches near the end of the book, chs. 38–41).

First, God wants to be known as a just God (40:8). Second, God is willing to allow humanity to create a better system of justice if it can (vv. 9-14). Third, God keeps his explanation of the reasons for many types of suffering to himself. Humanity needs to accept the fact that it is ignorant about many of the causes of suffering and learn to live with the fact that God is sometimes very mysterious (42:2-6; for further discussion of this topic, → sermon below, "God as Just," p. 126).

Possible Sermon Titles: "Does God Pervert Justice?" "Can Reeds Thrive without Water?" "Where Can Hope Be Found?" "Bildad the Traditionalist"

2. The Wicked Die Suddenly and Are Remembered No More (Job 18)

By this point in the story, the tension has increased considerably. The participants are starting to attack each other's character rather than deal with the substance of their arguments. It is obvious in Bildad's second speech that he is very angry at Job. He felt that Job had treated the friends like stupid animals. They had presented to him the wisdom of the ages, the best advice from the best thinkers of all time. But Job would not listen to them. Rather, he railed against them and against God. His arrogance was detestable.

As Bildad saw it, Job had only himself to blame for his predicament. He was well aware that Job had suffered terribly. But Job was only aggravating the situation by going off on his emotional tirades. These were hypocritical attempts to divert attention away from his own wrongdoing and direct it toward God as the culprit.

In their second speeches, all three friends tried to point out the terrible consequences that fall on those who pursue wickedness. In chapter 15, Eliphaz mentioned numerous examples, such as emotional turmoil, the loss of one's possessions, the loss of family members, and an early death for the sinner. Bildad agreed with all of that, but he chose a different emphasis. His concern was to point out (1) the suddenness and unexpectedness of death and (2) the consequences of wickedness that continue even after death.

Very creatively, Bildad describes some of the traps that hunters used to capture birds and wild animals. They included nets, covered pits in the ground, and nooses that grabbed an animal's leg when the trap was sprung. These traps were terribly frightening to the animals. They could be walking down a familiar path when suddenly they were caught in a trap and their freedom taken away. They knew their death was imminent. Similarly, God produces terror in the hearts of the wicked when he suddenly snatches them away from this world and sends them to Sheol.

Bildad also creates a very imaginative scenario of death's pursuit of the wicked. He personifies Death as a ruler, calling him "the king of terrors" (18:14). Death employs agents such as "dark[ness]," "trap[s]," "terrors," "calamity," and "disaster" (vv. 5-12) that he sends out into the world to terrorize the wicked. Once his agents have done their dirty work of frightening the wicked, then Death sends his "firstborn" named Disease (v. 13) to ravage their bodies before marching them off to Sheol.

Even after death, God's attack against the wicked continues (vv. 15-21). Their houses and lands are destroyed. Their possessions are burned up. And their children are all killed so that no one is left to preserve their memory. Thus life goes on without them. It is as if they never existed.

Bildad was the one who brought up Job's children in his first speech. There he suggested that Job's children may have caused their own deaths by sinning. Here in his second speech he points his finger at Job himself for causing his children's death. Bildad is convinced that one of the punishments experienced by wicked parents is the loss of their "offspring." So they have no one to carry on their family name (18:17, 19). Again, Job is hounded by a very cruel critic who uses personal attacks to defend his rigid understanding of the wisdom theology.

What can we learn from Bildad's scathing attacks against Job? This might be the appropriate place for preachers to examine the strengths and weaknesses of the traditionalist mindset.

Traditionalists typically are people who draw their inspiration from the past. They hold that *the good old days* provided all the guidance and resources one needs for the present. Great thinkers and sages of the past have already settled all the major issues of life. They created "a closed body of knowledge" (Newsom 1996, 405) that needs no further examination or refinement. The traditionalist thinks that the best way to live now is to be guided by the truths discovered by seekers after wisdom in previous generations.

Traditionalists are sometimes criticized as being old fashioned and out of touch. But in reality, the world needs traditionalists to remind us of the great lessons that were learned in the past. Otherwise we would be doomed to repeat the mistakes of prior generations. The world also needs creative and unmuzzled thinkers to help us in dealing with new problems in the present and future. Both types of people make valuable contributions to society. To emphasize one to the detriment of the other inevitably leads to societal turmoil.

The church also needs traditionalists. The contemporary church is continually impacted by the influences of politics, nationalism, and racism, as well as changes in music styles, discoveries in science, technological developments, and fads in religion. There is a tremendous need for traditionalists to continually remind the church of its biblical roots, its theological foundations, its long history of living out a Christlike lifestyle, and its powerful message of hope to a world that is often confused and disoriented.

At the same time, focusing entirely on the past soon creates ruts that are unattractive, out of touch, and ingrown. Changes in society demand new approaches from the church. New ways of thinking are needed within the body of Christ to develop new methods of reaching sinners with the gospel and to address the challenging issues of each generation. Maintaining a healthy balance between traditionalists and creative thinkers will always be a difficult but much-needed task for each new generation of God's people.

In Bildad's case, his main problem was not with his traditionalist mindset. In the history of humanity many traditionalists have guided communities through troubling times by pointing them back to proven principles that guided them in the past. Rather, Bildad's problems arose from (1) his ignorance of the divine conversation in the prologue, (2) his total reliance on the wisdom theology to explain all experiences of suffering, and (3) his arrogant belief in his own rightness. As a result, his emphasis on the suddenness of death for the wicked was totally irrelevant to Job's situation. Job was right to resist Bildad's suggestions.

III. Job 4-27: The Three Friends

Possible Sermon Titles: "The Lamp of the Wicked Is Suddenly Snuffed Out," "The Way of the Wicked," "Coming to Terms with the King of Terrors," "The Traditionalist Mindset: Out of Touch or Valuable Resource?"

3. "Dominion and Awe Belong to God" (Job 25; 24:18-24)

In several places in the book, Job expresses a desire to meet with God. One such passage (23:3-7) is located immediately before Bildad's third speech. Job believed very strongly that he was innocent of sin and not deserving of divine punishment. Therefore, his own suffering was totally undeserved. God had treated him unjustly. If a meeting between himself and God could be arranged, he believed he could prove his innocence. He believed his case was strong enough to convince God that God had made a mistake in punishing him.

Bildad thinks this is nonsense. And in his final speech he attacks this very point by reminding Job of some things that Eliphaz said much earlier. First, God is far more powerful than humanity (25:2-3). Not even all humanity collectively comes anywhere close to the power of God. "Dominion and awe belong" only to the Almighty (v. 2). Bildad is absolutely correct on this point, for God will stress its importance in his magnificent speech near the end of the book (chs. 38–41).

Second, God is far more "pure" and "righteous" than humanity (25:4-6). Compared to God's holiness, humankind is as morally dirty as "a maggot" (v. 6). So how can anyone claim to be righteous in comparison to God? And could Job ever hope to prove his moral innocence to one as holy as God? Eliphaz had already made this point in 4:17-21. Apparently Bildad felt it was important enough to bear repeating.

The implication of all of this is that the great divide between the divine and the human is too great for humanity to voice a complaint. Here is another passage where you can speak on the transcendence of God (see also 4:17–5:1).

In summary, we might compare Bildad to a modern college professor who has studied his field of knowledge for many years and gained expertise in its history, its premises and principles, its discoveries, and its importance and contributions to humanity. These professors are experts in their field. The main criticism of such individuals is that they fail to see the big picture because they are so narrowly focused on their discipline.

Such was the case with Bildad. Once he had finished his dissertation, "The Value of Being a Traditionalist," he had refrained from thinking a new, creative thought. The sages of previous generations had solved all the problems of life, and his dissertation had proven that. There were simply no unanswered questions left. He saw his responsibility now as serving God, following the advice of the sages before him, and teaching others in the ways of wisdom, not debating issues such as the justice of God. Bildad's strength was his unashamed devotion to the past. But it was also his weakness, for it hindered his ability to objectively evaluate Job's situation and provide the kind of comfort he really needed.

Possible Sermon Titles: "Only Maggots in Comparison to God," "Professor Bildad"

Zophar (Job 11, 20; 27:13-23)

1. Oh, That God Would Speak to You! (Job 11)

All three friends, as well as Job, were quite dogmatic in their speeches. They were each convinced that they were speaking the truth. Yet even more than the others, Zophar was the real dogmatist among them. It was his method of reasoning that gave him this designation. Whereas Eliphaz appealed to mystical visions and Bildad to the ancient wisdom traditions of the sages, Zophar based his arguments on logical lines of deductive reasoning that made good sense to him. He calls on Job to think as he does and agree with him. And he refuses to back down from his position, once stated.

In addition, Zophar presents his ideas in a blunt, critical, callous, and accusatory manner. He jumps right into attacking Job at the beginning of his first speech and never lessens the volume. His tactless, sarcastic put-down of Job in 11:12 is the most notable example of his harsh arrogance and bluster. It is obvious that he thinks Job is a fool.

Zophar's speech begins with a criticism of Job's claims of purity. Job never actually used the word "pure" (v. 4) to describe his spiritual condition. But for all intents and purposes he might as well have, for Job was absolutely certain that he was "innocent" and "blameless" of any sinful thought or activity (9:15, 20-21). And he believed that God agreed with him (10:7).

Faced with such a confident attitude, Zophar believed that his best line of attack was, first, to emphasize God's awesome wisdom and power (11:7-11) and, second, to describe the terrible punishments that God imposes on the wicked (20:4-29; 27:13-23). Using a series of metaphors, he describes God's knowledge as "higher," "deeper," "longer," and "wider" than any human can imagine (11:8-9). Thus God's actions cannot be comprehended by humankind. They are far above human levels of thinking. They remain a mystery that cannot be fathomed.

And God's power is just as awesome. Sinners cannot hide their evil deeds from God's awareness. And when he sees their sins, he imposes the judgment due. By speaking this way, Zophar hoped to convince Job that God is totally just in his dealings with humankind. Job's claims that God was unjust to him were erroneous.

Zophar then drives home his cynicism of Job's claims of moral innocence with a proverb about the impossibility of Job ever gaining a correct understanding of his situation (v. 12). The proverb was meant to criticize Job's continual babbling. To Zophar, Job sounded like a fool who did not even recognize his own ignorance.

Zophar knew that he and his friends were not making any headway in breaking down Job's defenses. And so in desperation he shouts out a wish that God would speak to Job. "Oh, that God would speak to you and straighten out your confused thinking" (vv. 5-6, author paraphrase)!

Have not each of us wished for something similar in the midst of a heated debate on a religious topic? Maybe we have not said anything out loud, but we certainly have thought it. When our arguments are not making any impression on an opposing party, we wish that the Ultimate Authority on the matter would step forward and clear the air of all false claims and faulty reasoning. But alas, it is a futile wish, for God usually chooses to remain silent in such situations.

Actually, God rarely intervenes in human activities in such a direct and public way, even though people have been asking him to do so for thousands of years. The priests and scribes asked such a question of Jesus while he was hanging on the cross: "Show us some signs so 'that we may see and believe' [NIV] in you" (Mark 15:31-32). However, that never has been God's method of trying to convince humankind of his truth.

So when Zophar expressed his wish that God suddenly appear and correct Job's ignorance, he knew this was not going to happen. But he says it anyway out of total frustration at his ineffectiveness in arguing with Job. And then he adds a pointed, sarcastic jab at Job (Job 11:6). "You know, Job, God has already been much kinder to you than you deserve. Fortunately for you he has not punished you to the full extent

III. Job 4-27: The Three Friends

of your sins. You think you are suffering now, but you have only experienced a small part of God's judgment that he could inflict on you. Thank God that so far he has been very merciful to you."

One gets the impression here that Zophar is not really bothered by the fact that God is not likely to appear to straighten out Job. He seems to think he already knows the mind of God. His intent is to enlighten Job on exactly what God would say if he did show up.

In verses 13-19, Zophar offers Job a word of hope, just as his companions Eliphaz and Bildad had done in their first speeches. He describes four conditions that God requires of people before he will change their situation (vv. 13-14). They are (1) "devote your heart" to God, (2) "stretch out your hands to God," (3) "put away the sin that is in your hand," and (4) "allow no evil to dwell in your tent." If Job would meet God's conditions, God would remove his miserable suffering and restore his life of integrity and blessing. It would be a magnificent divine reversal, just as astounding as going from darkness to light (v. 17).

Most people have wished at some point in their lives that God would work a divine reversal for them. This is why Zophar's words are so enticing. People sometimes pray fervent prayers for God to work a miracle for them by reversing the dreadful circumstances in which they find themselves. Maybe the request concerns healing from a dreaded disease, for release from a hated job, for reconciliation in a relationship that has gone sour, or for extra money to pay the bills. The list of human needs and requests is unending. The good news is that sometimes God answers those prayers. The bad news is that sometimes God does not. No one has yet figured out why God sometimes acts and why other times he remains silent.

Zophar thought that Job would see his prayers answered if he met the four conditions listed above (vv. 13-14), but he was wrong. Job had already met Zophar's conditions, and yet he still suffered. The same is still true today. Being in a right relationship with God and living a life of love and faithfulness do not guarantee health, wealth, and good relationships with others. As Jesus said, we will always have tribulations (John 16:33). The main benefit is the encouragement and stamina that God provides to carry on through life's trials. Just being in the presence of God provides the reassurance that we will be able to conquer life's battles (Deut. 31:6; Josh. 1:5, 9; Matt. 6:25-34; Rom. 8:35-39; Heb. 13:5).

However, there is one area of life where God does guarantee a divine reversal to anyone who asks. The possibility of our spiritual salvation from sin is a matter of deep concern to God. He has promised that if we will meet his conditions of confession, repentance, and faith, he will work the most magnificent transformation in each of our lives that we could ever imagine (John 3:16; 1 John 1:7, 9). Jesus described this reversal to Nicodemus as like being "born again" (John 3:7). And later to the crowds in Jerusalem, he said it was like going from "darkness" to "light" (8:12; 12:46). Paul explained it to the Corinthian church as becoming a "new creation" (2 Cor. 5:17).

In this one area of life, God does promise to reverse the darkness and gloom of sin and establish the light of salvation in its place. But in the other areas of life, such as health and wealth, there is no guarantee of a change. As Balentine notes, "The faithful must learn to 'trust and obey'" (2006, 194).

In the concluding portion of his speech, Zophar takes up the subject of hope, a topic all three friends comment on in their first speeches. They recognized that Job was devoid of hope and that this needed to be addressed before Job could turn his life around (see Bowes 2018, 186-87). Eliphaz offered hope to Job based on his former exemplary life and on God's nature, which always rewards those who are truly righteous. Bildad, too, offered hope, pointing out that God never rejects the blameless. Zophar adds to this chorus of hope by emphasizing the many benefits experienced by those who turn to God. People who seek God and quit sinning are blessed by God in so many ways (Job 11:13-19).

So each friend in turn presents Job with good reasons to seek God and be reconciled with him. But you get the feeling that none of them really believe Job will listen to them. And this is borne out in each of their second speeches. After listening to Job's rejection of their offers of hope, they have nothing but criticism and judgment to present in the second cycle (chs. 15, 18, 20).

The mention of hope, though, does open up a door for contemporary followers of God to consider the source of hope in their own lives. Where is hope to be found today? In a world that experiences so much tragedy, sorrow, corruption, and fear, is hope even possible? Or are we doomed to a life of trouble and uncertainty? And closely tied to that question is the question of God's justice. For if God rendered observable justice in all situations in the world, would this world not be in much better shape than it is now? Would we not have more hope if every sinner were punished and every righteous person were rewarded?

III. Job 4–27: The Three Friends

Here you can describe Job's brief comments on hope (9:33-35; 16:19-21; 19:25-27; → also the sermon below, "Three Brief Glimpses of Hope," p. 88) and then focus on NT contributions to the subject of hope using passages such as John 14–15. The NT provides a new source of hope through Christ that OT writers never considered. Our present hope is grounded in two things: (1) in the faithfulness of God who has demonstrated time and time again his love and care for humanity and (2) in the work of Christ, who provided the means of salvation and the promise of eternal life. And this hope is facilitated and encouraged through daily fellowship with the Holy Spirit. Even in the midst of the troubles of life, such hope is possible for those who believe (1 Pet. 1:3-9).

Possible Sermon Titles: "Oh, That God Would Speak to You!" "Where Is Hope to Be Found?" "Zophar the Dogmatist"

2. God's Sudden Reversals (Job 20; 27:13-23)

All through Scripture we find stories of God's sudden reversal of situations in life. Sometimes these stories portray God as a deliverer, dramatically rescuing his people from a hopeless situation. For example, there is the parting of the Red Sea allowing the Israelites to escape from the Egyptian army (Exod. 14:21-31) and Peter's release from prison (Acts 12:1-11). Eliphaz emphasized this aspect of God's character in his first speech (Job 5:11, 15-16, 18-26).

Other times, God suddenly reverses the well-being of the wicked, causing their death or the loss of their family, possessions, and health. Two well-known examples are Haman's demise (Esther 7:1-10) and Herod Agrippa I's sudden death (Acts 12:19-23). None of these reversals were the result of coincidence. They were actions taken by God when deemed necessary to right wrongs or punish specific evildoers. God's justice lies at the heart of these situations.

The description of God as a punisher of sin is mentioned by all three friends. But Zophar especially made it a central theme of his second and third speeches. For him, the wicked may look successful for a time. They may accumulate great wealth and rise to high positions of power and influence. But at some point in this life, God will bring his terrible judgment against them. He will remove their power and wealth and send them to an early grave. According to Zophar, this is the way God desires

III. Job 4-27: The Three Friends

to treat the wicked (Job 20:29), and this is the way he has always functioned (vv. 4-5).

In verses 4-29, Zophar presents a number of metaphors illustrating God's sudden reversals in the lives of the wicked. One example is the sudden loss of joy by the godless (v. 5). Another is their sudden disappearance, like the dream that vanishes upon awakening (vv. 7-9). A third is the unexpected change from sweetness to poisonous venom (vv. 12-14). Wickedness is like sweet candy that tastes delicious in the mouth. But after one has swallowed it, the candy turns to poison in the stomach. A fourth is the total destruction of the possessions of the wicked by fire or flood (vv. 26, 28). Perhaps the best phrasing of this sudden reversal in the lives of the wicked appears in 27:19: "He lies down wealthy, but will do so no more; when he opens his eyes, all is gone."

What is so sad about Zophar's attempt to counsel Job is that he never mentions Job's comment in his last speech about Job's hope for a redeemer (19:25-27). If he had been listening to Job instead of plotting how to attack Job in his next speech, he could easily have enlarged on that thought and pointed to God's ability to reverse Job's situation for the good. Instead, he focused on God's power to reverse the good times for sinners. The wicked are doomed. It is only a matter of time until they exit this world, for their fate is sealed.

One of the questions Zophar's speeches raise is, Does God really punish people for sin? The answer from both Testaments is yes. The OT certainly supports the concept that God punishes sin (Deut. 28:15-68), and so does the apostle Paul (Rom. 2:6; for further discussion, see Bowes 2018, 120-21).

However, some scholars are uncomfortable with this description of God. They would rather attribute only goodness and love to God and place the blame for sin's consequences on human beings themselves (as in Ps. 7:15 [16 HB]). The nature of sin is such that its consequences are known and inevitable. People who choose a life of sin are causing their own destruction.

A careful study of the OT reveals that both answers to this question are correct. (1) On the one hand, God does cause people to suffer for their sins. He brings judgment on the wicked, proving that he is a just God (Gen. 3:14-19; 6:5-7, 13; Pss. 11:6; 145:20; Prov. 21:12; Isa. 11:4; 13:11; Jer. 25:31). The Jewish exile in Babylonia is a good example. (2) On the other hand, bad consequences are naturally associated with sin.

III. Job 4–27: The Three Friends

When people choose to sin, they are choosing the consequences that are connected with it. So they cause their own downfall and suffering (Pss. 7:15 [16 HB]; 9:16 [17 HB]; 141:10; Prov. 11:5).

The fact that both answers in the previous paragraph are supported in Scripture would indicate that some combination of both must be the correct interpretation. The story of the fall in Gen. 2:16-17; 3:1-24 makes this clear. In the beginning, God created a moral universe that required human beings to make moral choices for good or for evil. And those moral choices came with consequences that were made known ahead of time. God specifically told Adam and Eve what *he* would do to them if they ignored or defied his boundaries. So they knew the consequences connected with bad choices. When they did disobey, God imposed on the first couple the punishment of which he had warned them. Thus, in different ways, both God and humans are each responsible for whatever bad consequences are experienced as a result of sin.

Fortunately for Adam and Eve, they also experienced God's mercy. God gave them additional years of life, although under difficult circumstances. And so do we experience God's mercy, for which we all are thankful.

At this point, the sermon could easily move in the direction of enlightening the congregation on a proper theology of sin. Questions such as the following could be addressed: (1) What is sin? (2) How did sin originate? (3) How has sin affected human beings both internally and in their social relationships? (4) How does one's theology of sin affect one's understanding of the afterlife? (5) What is God's remedy for sin—both the acts of sin and inherited sin? (6) How can one be freed from sin right now? (7) In what ways does one's life change when freed from sin?

The topic of sin is not frequently mentioned from contemporary pulpits. As a result, there is a great deal of muddled thinking in the minds of many churchgoers. And a misunderstanding of sin will likely result in a misunderstanding of the nature of God and salvation. A good, solid message that defines sin, lays out its causes and consequences, and points people to God's plan of salvation should be a goal of every preacher on a regular basis.

Possible Sermon Titles: "Divine Reversals Are Sometimes a Part of God's Plans," "Does God Really Punish People for Sin?" "What Is Sin and How Can I Be Rid of It?"

IV. JOB 4-27: JOB'S RESPONSES TO HIS FRIENDS

Job's Condition

Before presenting the content of Job's speeches, you might consider providing the congregation with a general description of Job's condition and overall state of mind. This is needed as background because he says some very strange things that do not seem to correlate with his super-saint image in the prologue. The congregation needs to know what was driving Job to speak as he does. The following points can be emphasized.

1. Job Was Experiencing Intense Physical Pain

The skin disease inflicted by the Examiner (2:7-8) continued to fester for many months. The black scabs now covering his body (30:30) broke open regularly and oozed pus. Some areas were even infected with worms (7:5). His body was reduced to skin and bones (19:20), and it burned with a fever (30:30). He suffered constant pain (v. 17). Imagine what it would be like to experience all of this with no access to modern pain-killing drugs. Could a person even think clearly in the midst of this terrible agony?

In addition, he was physically exhausted. He could not sleep at night because God kept terrifying him with nightmares (7:4, 13-14). And during the day, he could not refrain from weeping over his despicable condition (16:16).

IV. Job 4-27: Job's Responses to His Friends

Because of his physical pain, Job fully expected to die very shortly (6:8-9; 7:6-10, 21; 17:1, 13-16). He was certainly not making long-range plans for retirement. Rather, he thought he might die within a matter of weeks. Keep in mind that ancient people had very little knowledge about the causes of disease. They thought that severe pain probably indicated that a disease was terminal.

Job was so miserable that he wanted God to take his life immediately. Even though he had nothing to look forward to in Sheol, he believed it would provide relief from his suffering. But he had one last request to make of God. He wanted God to leave him alone so he could have some peace in his final moments (7:16; 10:20-22). God had been so cruel and unjust to him that he wanted to spend his final moments by himself—just himself and his thoughts pondering over the meaning of a wasted and senseless life.

Job was definitely thinking about death and planning for it. He could not avoid this topic because it seemed to be approaching very rapidly. So all of Job's remarks should be viewed as coming from someone on his deathbed.

2. Job Was Experiencing Intense Emotional Pain

Job certainly appreciated the presence of his three friends, for no one other than his wife had dared to console him or even approach him. Both family and community kept their distance. But after listening to the friends through several speeches, Job was convinced that his friends were worthless counselors. He called them "plasterers of deception" (AT) and "worthless physicians" (13:4). They claimed they were there to comfort him, but only Eliphaz treated him kindly, and then only in his first speech (chs. 4–5). The rest of the speeches from the friends were rather harsh. They expressed no empathy for his plight. They were only interested in advancing their own agendas.

At times Job lashes out at his friends because he felt they were undependable. They were like streams that seemed to offer fresh water, but they dried up as soon as the spring rains ceased (6:15-17). They also offered him false hope that he would one day be restored, but they based their analysis on old principles of the wisdom theology that did not apply to him. He was already doing everything they told him to do. On one occasion Job offered to shut up and let them teach him (v. 24), but they only responded with the same old advice.

IV. Job 4-27: Job's Responses to His Friends

What made Job extremely angry was their refusal to even consider his own testimony. They were not interested in his thoughts because they believed he was hiding something from them. And they thought he was too young to understand the true ways of life. Because they were so rigidly locked into their own principles, they were useless in helping Job sort out all of the conflicting evidence he tried to present to them.

Further, the people in Job's community no longer wanted him around. His reputation had once been sterling (ch. 29). He had sat with the elders at the gate of the city as a sign of honor. His advice was highly respected. And he sought to raise the welfare of his community by financially supporting anyone who was poor or needy. But overnight, his respectability vanished. Now his community mocked him, even spitting in his face (17:6). They used his name as a byword for what happens to people when they turn against God (30:9). They were now warning each other: "You better not sin against God, or you will end up just like Job." They treated him as if he were cursed. No one wanted to be seen with him (19:13-19).

As a consequence, Job felt totally isolated from other human beings. His whole social network of family and friends had collapsed around him. This completely drained him of any normal human emotions that arise through healthy relationships and helps explain some of his harsh words to his friends. He desperately wanted comfort, but no one was willing to give him a hug. So all of Job's remarks need to be viewed as coming from someone who had no real friends left in this world.

3. Job Was Experiencing Intense Spiritual Pain

Job believed with all his heart that he was in a right relationship with God. He was willing to admit that he might have committed some youthful sin when he was much younger (13:26). But his conscience was now clear that all past sins had been forgiven and that he was absolutely blameless before God. We, the readers of this book, know that Job was correct in his belief. Both the author and God himself confirm multiple times in the prologue that Job was innocent of any sin (1:1, 8, 22; 2:3, 10).

Further, Job was prepared to defend himself against any other person and even against God to prove his spiritual blamelessness. He had a speech all ready to deliver, and he knew it would prove his innocence (13:18). His only problem was that he could not convince God to show up for a debate (23:1-9). God refused to talk with him, even though Job had pleaded for an audience (13:20-24). And so Job was confused about what was happening to him. Why did God remain silent? Why had he abandoned his favorite saint? In Job's thinking, God's silence could only mean that he was trying to avoid Job. And the physical pain Job was enduring could only mean that God was angry at him. God was punishing him for no good reason and now regarded Job as his enemy. Job even felt as if he were a target at which God was shooting (6:4; 7:12-20; 9:17-19; 10:2-17; 13:24; 19:7-12).

We, the readers, know this was not true. But neither Job nor his friends were privy to this information. We know Job's suffering had nothing to do with sin or punishment. It was a divine test of his motivation for righteousness. But because Job lived in an environment that believed all suffering was due to sin, he could not shake this belief. And neither could his three friends. It was what all ancient people had been taught by their forefathers for centuries.

There are still people today who fall prey to this way of thinking. But it is a superstition, not a fact. And the book of Job proves it has no factual evidence to support it. Unfortunately, it is a very harmful superstition that has created many doubts in the minds of good people about the love and goodness of God.

But whether right or wrong, this was the belief system within which Job was operating. And it raised profound questions in his mind about his faith. If he was extremely righteous, and he was, why was he suffering so severely? He should be experiencing God's blessings instead of his curses. The only explanation that made sense to him was that he was suffering unjustly.

But this raised an even more troublesome issue. This meant that God was unjust, for God caused all things to happen (21:22-26). Job shuddered to think that this might be true, for the whole wisdom theology of the sages rejected it. But it was the only logical explanation he could think of. God was unjust in his treatment of Job. Therefore, he must be unjust in his treatment of others, too, for Job had lived long enough to know that the wicked often get away with murder and that the righteous often experience trouble and pain (ch. 21).

Job was lost spiritually. The lighthouses on the shore that he had depended on in the past for orientation had now gone out. He felt "hedged in" by the circumstances of life that God had forced him to endure (3:23).

IV. Job 4-27: Job's Responses to His Friends

4. Job Had Lost All Hope

All of the pain mentioned above created a vacuum in Job's heart that cried out for answers, especially answers from God. When God refused to provide him with those answers, Job lost all hope (7:6).

The word "hope" appears frequently in the book of Job. The friends seemed to have easy explanations for obtaining hope in this life, for they assumed that the righteous never suffer. "Serve God," they said, "and you will be blessed abundantly." But Job knew differently, and so his comments about hope are generally pessimistic. For him, a "tree" that has been cut off leaving only a "stump" has a greater possibility of reviving than does a human being who has been "laid low" by the misfortunes of life (14:7-10). Job's suffering had convinced him that there was no hope in this life (vv. 18-22). And so he had resigned himself to a life without "happiness" (7:7). "Bitterness" now engulfed his soul (7:11; 10:1). He despised his life (7:16) and wished he were dead (10:18-19). He wanted to die quickly and find rest in Sheol (6:8-9).

What is so sad about Job's lack of hope is that he projected his own problems onto everyone else. He believed that all human beings live miserable lives. We experience the same type of suffering and injustice that God inflicted on Job. We all are "of few days and full of trouble" (14:1; see Ps. 90:10 for a similar comment). We "spring up like flowers," fresh and beautiful in the morning, but by the end of the day we have withered away to nothing (Job 14:2).

Job uses a number of similes to reinforce his belief in the hopelessness of life. He compares our desire to die to a "slave" longing for the day's work to end (7:2). The unsubstantial nature of life is compared to a "breath" of air (v. 7) or a "cloud" that quickly vanishes (v. 9). The swiftness of our existence on earth is like the speed of a "weaver's shuttle" (v. 6) or that of a "runner" on land (9:25) or a "papyrus" boat on the water or a swooping "eagle" in the air (v. 26). For Job, we appear briefly in life, live out our appointed number of days while experiencing great suffering, and then quickly disappear into oblivion. Whether we are righteous or sinful does not really matter. God treats all human beings the same (v. 22).

Is Job correct in his evaluation of life? Before offering a hasty answer, one needs to ponder deeply the trouble and pain that humans experience. Disease, war, natural disasters, and human cruelty to one another are ever present and have always been so. But is the human condition so

IV. Job 4-27: Job's Responses to His Friends

miserable that there is no value in living (ch. 14)? Is our world so mixed up, and is God so unjust in his dealings with human beings that uncertainty and chaos are the only things we can count on in life (in addition to taxes and death)? If you were in Job's situation, what song would you be singing: "I've got a mansion just over the hilltop"* or "You load sixteen tons, what do you get? Another day older and deeper in debt"?†

This sermon seems pretty dire, and it is. But sometimes a person needs to flush all of the silliness and superficiality out of life and entertain some serious thoughts about his or her present spiritual condition. Life can seem pretty boring and meaningless without some sense of direction and purpose and hope.

The conclusion to this sermon should focus on words of challenge for the next Sunday's sermon: "Do you have hope today, and if so, why? What is the source of hope for you? How have you been able to maintain your hope and live a meaningful life in the midst of a chaotic world? These are profound questions that we will attempt to answer in the next sermon. Please spend some time thinking about them this week. And it might be helpful to discuss them with a spouse or parent or friend."

Possible Sermon Titles: "Hopeless in Uz," "Less Hope Than a Tree Stump?" "A Miserable Human Being"

Three Brief Glimpses of Hope (Job 9, 16, 19)

The previous sermon examined the reasons for Job's lack of hope. His overall view of life was that things would never get better for him. But there are actually three places in the dialogues where Job expresses a tiny smidgen of hope. They are as follows.

1. Job Wished for a Mediator

Job's first hopeful comments appear in 9:33. In the first part of chapter 9, Job commented on the greatness of God. God is awesomely powerful in his relationship with the world. He created the heavens and arranged the star constellations into their various forms. He causes

---

*Ira Stanphill, "Mansion over the Hilltop," Copyright © 1949 (renewed) by Singspiration, Inc. All rights reserved.
†Merle Travis, "Sixteen Tons," Copyright © 1947 by Unichappell Music, Inc., and Elvis Presley Music. Copyright renewed. All rights reserved.

IV. Job 4-27: Job's Responses to His Friends

earthquakes and eclipses of the sun. His "wonders" in nature are unfathomable by humanity, and his "miracles" are so numerous they cannot be counted (v. 10).

In short, God does whatever he pleases and goes wherever he wants. No one can stop him. In fact, because God is invisible, no one even knows when he is around so they can complain or ask a question. His mighty power and the wisdom to use it overwhelm any human being who wishes to challenge him.

Therefore, Job feels at a decided disadvantage in trying to confront God with questions about his own suffering. How is he supposed to go about it? Even if he is totally blameless, he is afraid that God will just ignore him as unworthy of his attention. Or God will get angry and crush the life out of him. He believes that God does not want to be challenged about his justice or lack thereof in this world. God just wants everything done his way without any questions asked. So what chance does a finite human being have in arguing with God, even if that human being has a solid, airtight case to present?

Job's first hopeful comment concerns the possibility of using a mediator to bring about reconciliation between himself and God (v. 33). This mediator would have knowledge of both the divine and the human and be skilled in negotiation. This person would be neutral—someone who would listen fairly to both parties and not take sides. A mediator might be able to point out faulty lines of reasoning and suggest reasonable solutions and compromises. And Job would not have to fear talking to a mediator, as he feared talking to omnipotent God. He would not even have to come into God's presence and be overwhelmed by God's awesome power, for the mediator could relay messages back and forth between himself and God without them even seeing each other. In short, Job felt that a mediator was just what he needed to resolve his differences with God.

The type of mediator Job describes is fairly common in our world today. Mediators have been successful in preventing divorces, resolving labor disputes, and even deterring war between countries. Mediators can be invaluable in arbitrating all types of conflicts.

But almost as soon as the words were out of his mouth, Job knew that his idea was not workable. No such divine-human being existed, as far as he knew. Even angels could not perform that role (5:1). Consequently, his first attempt at resolution was short lived, and he fell back into his depression.

In NT theology Jesus Christ is regarded as the divine-human mediator for the sins of all humanity. But Jesus's role is not what Job desired. Job was not sinful and, therefore, not requesting for someone to provide a means for his salvation from sin. Rather, he was confused about the reasons for his suffering. Since God had not spoken to him directly, he wanted someone to speak to God for him and to arbitrate their differences.

2. Job Believed He Had a Witness

Job's second word of hope concerns a "witness" (16:19). What Job means is a person who fully supports his side and will advocate for him. This person is completely different from the mediator he requested in 9:33. There he was thinking of someone like an umpire or a referee who remains neutral to the two sides in a sports contest. Here in 16:19-20 Job is thinking of someone much more friendly to him. Like a witness in a court case, Job's witness would know every detail of his life and be able to vouch for its accuracy. Also, unlike the mediator whose existence he doubted, Job is much more confident that his witness does exist.

There has been much discussion among scholars trying to identify Job's witness (see Bowes 2018, 224-25). Who is this person? One suggestion is that it is not a person at all. It is heaven in general. In the verse prior to his mention of a witness, Job called on the earth to keep the memory of his life alive. So even if he died, his reputation and innocence could still be proven (v. 18). And then in verse 19, he identifies heaven as the location of his witness.

Sometimes people in the OT appealed to both the earth and the heavens to testify on their behalf about a specific claim (Deut. 4:26; 30:19; 31:28; 32:1; Jer. 6:19; Mic. 1:2). The reason was because these two entities see and know everything that happens. So it is very possible that Job may be calling on earth and heaven to support the truthfulness of his claims against God.

However, another possibility is that Job is identifying God himself as his witness. Even though he believes that God has caused his suffering and treated him unjustly, yet God is the only one who knows everything about him. For this reason, God would be an excellent witness of his innocence. In effect, Job is issuing God a subpoena to prod him into stating the truth about Job's innocence. By doing so, he is attempting to require God to come to his defense with the honest truth when and if his case ever comes up.

IV. Job 4-27: Job's Responses to His Friends

It is true that this interpretation sets up a conflict between God as judge, as defendant, and as witness. But perhaps God's complex and infinite nature would allow all three when viewed from different perspectives (see "God's Paradoxical Nature" in Bowes 2018, 225).

3. Job Was Confident He Had a Vindicator

Job's confidence regarding a "redeemer" (Job 19:25) is one of the highlights of the book. He is fully persuaded that this person exists and that at some point in the future this person will defend Job before God and secure his vindication. Those who are familiar with Handel's *Messiah* know that the part based on 19:25 is one of the most inspiring parts of that musical piece. But Handel applied the verse to Christ as the redeemer for all human sin.

In the book, Job was not even considering the need for redemption from sin. He was already sinless (1:1, 8; 2:3). His desire was for a "vindicator" (AT; a better translation) who would publicly prove Job's innocence and officially end any lingering suspicions that Job was being punished for sin. Job would have given anything to bring about the appearance of such a vindicator.

However, before getting to Job's confidence in a vindicator, there are some important verses immediately preceding this passage. In 19:23-24 Job expresses a deep longing for a permanent record to be made of all the events in his life. This recording would be inscribed on a large stone monument. Stone inscriptions were the way ancient kings made permanent records of their deeds and pronouncements because they lasted forever. Hundreds of these inscriptions from Egypt and Mesopotamia are still in existence today because they were inscribed on stone. The most well known are probably the Code of Hammurabi and the Egyptian hieroglyphs on the temples at Luxor and Karnak.

Job wanted a similar inscription because he was afraid he would die before God considered his case. A permanent written record was the only way he knew how to secure his vindication after his death. You might comment here on ways people seek permanency today, such as establishing foundations, endowing colleges, and putting their names on buildings.

However, Job's thoughts about a permanent record were only a wish because he had no way of producing such an inscription. So a better plan was for his vindicator to appear now and set the record straight about Job's innocence while he was still alive.

The vindicator Job was counting on is not identified in the passage. This has led to different interpretations. The most probable person is God, even though this creates some tension in the understanding of God's nature (as in no. 2 above). Job was convinced that only God knew all the details of his past history and present predicament. Only God knew the real reason why Job was suffering. And only God could officially avow Job's blamelessness. Consequently, he was depending on God to come to his rescue (1) by testifying to his basic sinlessness, (2) by revealing the real cause of his suffering, and (3) by restoring his honor and integrity in his community.

Job deeply desired that God would do these things right now. He desperately wanted to "see" God (19:27). By this he meant that he wanted a meeting with God before he died, and he wanted this meeting to result in reconciliation. He longed to fellowship with God again and receive God's approval and blessing. But he believed his death was imminent, and so he was frustrated and pessimistic that he would die before his vindication could be secured. His frustration is expressed in verses 25b-26a: "And at some point in the future he will stand upon the earth, and this, after my skin is stripped off" (AT). Job's confidence in the existence of his vindicator was tempered by his fear that this person would not show up before Job's death. Because of this, from his mountaintop of faith in verse 25a ("I know that my [vindicator] lives" [NIV]), Job slips back into his bitterness in chapter 21.

In conclusion, what is the answer to last week's question: Where can people find hope in the midst of a chaotic world? The answer is that they can find hope in the same place Job was looking. Job believed he could have used the help of a mediator, a witness, or a vindicator. But in the depths of his being, Job knew that only God had the right answers to his deepest questions and the right solution to his problems. So even though he felt that God was punishing him and refusing to talk with him, his attention on God never wavered.

The friends were definitely not looking for hope in the right place. They were too focused on their own agendas, which emphasized the ancient wisdom theology and some unknown sin Job may have committed. But Job's entire attention was centered on what God thought about his situation. He agreed with the author in 28:23 that God was the only one who could provide the kind of wisdom and hope needed for dealing with life's problems. Therefore, he kept going back to God and pleading for God to meet him. His hope was based on the possibility of a personal encounter with almighty God. And as we find out later in the book, God graciously granted him such a meeting. This is one of the most important lessons to be learned from this magnificent book.

For additional comments on the topic of hope, → the earlier sermon "Oh, That God Would Speak to You" (p. 75). A sermon on hope is a good topic for the Advent season.

Possible Sermon Titles: "I Know That My Redeemer Lives," "Three Words of Hope: Mediation, Testimony, and Vindication"

Taking God to Court (Job 9-10, 13, 19, 23)

Most adults have probably voiced a complaint to God at least once in their lifetime. "God, why did you do this?" or "God, why didn't you do this?" are common human complaints. So Job's complaining/whining spirit is not unique. What is unique is his desire to actually take God to court over God's supposed malpractice in causing Job's troubles.

Job was absolutely convinced that God was treating him unjustly (19:6). According to the wisdom of the time, Job's outstanding righteousness as described in 1:1-5 should have been noticed by God and rewarded with abundant blessing. Instead, God had taken away his wealth, his health, and his family (chs. 1–2).

Job goes into more detail about God's mistreatment in chapter 19. First, God had refused to answer his cries for help (v. 7). Even when Job screamed out that he was being violently wronged, God failed to come to his rescue. Second, God had obstructed and darkened his pathway (v. 8). Third, God had taken away the respect and honor he had formerly enjoyed in his community (v. 9). His reputation was now shattered. Fourth, God had destroyed any spark of life or hope in him (v. 10). Fifth, God was fiercely angry at him, treating him like an enemy (v. 11). And sixth, God had sent his agents (probably a subtle reference to the three friends) to surround and attack him (v. 12).

Job's final complaint in this chapter involved his family and friends. God had completely disrupted all of Job's former social relationships. Extended family, servants, guests, neighbors, close friends and colleagues, and even his wife were now avoiding any contact with him (vv. 13-19).

When one seriously ponders this list of complaints and begins to recognize the enormity of Job's suffering, it is easy to understand why Job wanted to take God to court. If God were truly guilty of all that Job had accused him of, then Job had a right not only to complain but also to bring charges. And he had justification for believing God would be found guilty, for the evidence strongly pointed toward the injustice of God's actions.

There are lots of questions about how this would all work out, since Job is placing God in the position of defendant as well as judge and, in another passage, as a witness for the prosecution (16:19). But Job does not seem concerned with the details of his plan, only that God needs to be called to account in some way for the misuse of his power in relation to Job.

Job expresses his idea of taking God to court specifically in chapters 9–10, with a few additional references in chapters 13 and 23. But even though he argues for the need to do this to God, he undercuts his own position by noting that all the power lies on God's side. Job knows he is puny compared to almighty God. He feels like an ordinary person with a few dollars in his bank account going up against an international corporate giant such as Bank of America. He makes the following comments about how mighty God is.

First, God's wisdom and power are so much greater than Job's (9:4). God can even cause earthquakes and eclipses (vv. 6-7). Second, God is creator of all (vv. 8-9). This gives him insights into the nature of things because he knows how they work. Third, God is invisible (v. 11). Job does not even know when God is present or where he can be located (23:3, 8-9). Fourth, God does whatever he wants to do (9:12; 23:13). No one can stop him or question his actions. Fifth, God likely would use his power to either overwhelm Job or ignore him (9:14-18). Therefore, Job reckoned that he was at a decided disadvantage in confronting God in a legal setting.

Nevertheless, in spite of God's vastly superior position in comparison to Job (v. 32), Job imagines in his mind what it would be like to take God to a court of law where the two of them could argue their cases as equals. His initial request was for a mediator to bring the two parties together and negotiate a fair settlement (vv. 33-35). But if mediation broke down and a real court case ensued, Job is fairly confident he could win his case (13:18; 23:10). He knows exactly what he would say to prove his innocence, and he believes God would exonerate him after listening

IV. Job 4-27: Job's Responses to His Friends

to him speak (13:15-18; 23:4-7). Most likely, chapters 29–31 contain the heart of what Job would say to God in a court case. They contain a description of Job's condition both before and after the calamities, and a strong oath of innocence.

Before we jump on Job's bandwagon and support his complaints as legitimate, we need to remember that Job was missing one crucial piece of evidence. He had not been privy to the heavenly conversation between God and the Examiner in chapters 1–2. Therefore, he had not heard God's words of praise for him. And he was ignorant of why God allowed the Examiner to treat him so cruelly. In fact, he did not even know that the Examiner existed in heaven. As a result, his charges against God were mistaken because his evidence was incomplete.

Such is the danger we all face when questioning God's actions in the world. None of us see the big picture, yet we act as if we do.

Surprisingly, God does allow his creatures to question his plans and doubt his wisdom. And some have dared to do so, such as Abraham (Gen. 18:23-33), Moses (Exod. 32:11-14; Num. 14:11-26), Elijah (1 Kings 19:1-18), and Jonah (Jon. 4). Times of great calamity and misery seem to bring forth a multitude of complaints against God. For example, the cries of anguish and bitterness in Lamentations 2:1–3:18 are a product of the destruction of Jerusalem. Similarly, in the twentieth century, the two World Wars and the Holocaust produced a number of writers who questioned God's wisdom and justice in the midst of so much suffering.

There are probably two reasons why God allows his creatures to question his judgment. The first springs out of the creation act itself. God created human beings with a free will and the freedom to reject God's plans for them. This indicates that God, even though he is sovereign, is not a dictator who punishes everyone who disagrees with him. He loves all human beings and desires to fellowship with them, and he makes every effort to do so. But he knows that some will exercise their free will in self-centered ways and reject his wisdom.

Second, God knows that his decision to withhold some information from humanity and thus maintain his free and mysterious nature inevitably produces doubts (Balentine 2006, 377-79). Doubts can only be swept away when there is complete transparency, and transparency is not one of God's characteristics. This statement is not intended to imply that God is dishonest, sneaky, underhanded, secretive, or up to no good. It is simply an acknowledgment that God has chosen not to reveal all the information about himself to his creation. Humans will always be in the dark about some things because God wants to keep it that way (for some of the possible reasons why God wishes to remain hidden, → the sermon below, "God as Free and Mysterious," p. 128).

Consequently, some questions and doubts are inevitable. This should encourage people to take their troubles and concerns to their Creator and begin an honest dialogue about how to understand and deal with them. The answers God gives may not be what we expect or what we think we need. But God will give us all the information he thinks is necessary. And he promises us his presence and his willingness to share the heavy load of our burdens (Matt. 11:28-30).

The friends viewed Job's doubts and complaints as a sign of moral rebellion, but Job regarded them as honest expressions of his confusion over God's intentions. God regarded them the same way. God was definitely displeased with some of Job's accusations, especially as they related to God's justice (Job 40:8-9). But he was willing to attribute them to a normal human reaction to intense pain.

Job's boldness in wanting to question God and challenge his treatment of human beings is far different from the usual approach to God found in the laments in the book of Psalms. There people pleaded with God for mercy. They requested immediate deliverance from the wicked (Ps. 10), from an enemy (Ps. 3), from a slanderer (Ps. 31), from a disease (Ps. 6), and so forth. They wanted God to right wrongs from the past and present and secure a stable, blessed life for them in the future.

But Job never directly asks God for healing from his skin disease or for the restoration of his possessions, family, and reputation. He seems much more interested in proving that God is unjust. Winning the intellectual battle with God and proving his innocence are far more important to Job than his own physical comfort (Job 27:2-6). He believes it is his right to point out God's inadequacies and teach him how to judge better (21:22-26). Job is realistic enough to know that the odds of ever winning a case against God are next to impossible (9:2-3). But that is not going to prevent him from trying. And so Job calls on heaven and earth to stand with him as witnesses to the truth of his innocence (16:18-19).

For a person to speak to God as Job speaks demands a great deal of integrity. The average followers of God are content to let the circumstances of life dictate their life's pathway while believing that God has an overall plan for their well-being. But Job was not the average person.

IV. Job 4-27: Job's Responses to His Friends

He was deeply disturbed that God had not treated him better. He felt and looked as if he were being punished as the worst of sinners. At the same time, his conscience was clear that he had not sinned against God. The internal anguish this produced was what drove Job to despair of ever enjoying life again. He regretted that he had ever been born (10:18). But Job's integrity would not let the matter rest. Others might consider it dangerous to challenge God on his treatment of individual human beings, but not Job. He wanted answers to his questions, and he knew that only God had those answers. His defense of his integrity in 27:2-6, which is supported later with specific examples in chapter 31, reveals that Job valued his integrity more than almost anything else.

Integrity is not a human quality that is always admired in society today. Pleasure, wealth, power, and popularity are sought after more often. When we look around us, we see that people of integrity do not always win elections. People of integrity are sometimes passed over as potential CEOs. And people of integrity may be shunned as friends because they are too honest. But people of integrity are apparently much admired by God.

Job wanted God's approval of his life more than anything else. No doubt, the commendation that Job received from God at the end of the book (42:8) was worth far more to him than any of the blessings that God later bestowed on him (vv. 12-17). So Job's desire to take God to court paid off. God recognized that Job was a serious man of integrity with serious questions about life. Even though God did not answer Job's questions, he recognized that Job was on the right track. His attention was focused in the right direction. God was extremely pleased with that.

For us, integrity is something we sometimes struggle with, for it demands a number of qualities such as courage, discipline, humility, honesty, and perseverance. The world does not always place a high value on these qualities, so not everyone desires to make the sacrifices that a life of integrity requires. Job was convinced that integrity was not just one way to live; it was the only way to live. Hopefully, his example will attract more to follow in his footsteps.

Possible Sermon Titles: "A Life of Integrity," "Challenging God in Court," "Doubts about God's Goodness and Wisdom," "A Malpractice Suit against God"

A Violent God (Job 16–17)

This is a sermon preachers should think long and hard about before entering the pulpit, for it takes us into one of the most difficult mazes of human understanding about God. And if we are honest, we know that when we exit this maze, we will not have any better grasp of the answer than when we entered. Because of this, many preachers will probably leave this topic out of their series on Job.

One cannot read the book of Job without noticing the strong language Job uses to describe God's treatment of him. Chapters 16–17 are especially relevant. Here Job accuses God of being a cruel monster. His evidence is as follows. God has attacked him relentlessly by destroying his family (16:7), by infecting his body with disease (v. 8), and by turning his community against him (vv. 10-11; 17:2, 6; 19:13-22). God treats him like an enemy, firing salvo after salvo of arrows into his body (16:12-13; 6:4; 7:20; 19:11). Like a lion pursuing its prey, God has fastened his eyes on Job and will not let Job out of his sight (16:9). God has attacked him and physically mauled him (v. 12). Job has even heard God angrily gnashing his teeth at him (v. 9).

In a later speech (ch. 30) Job adds further complaints about God's violent actions. God has grabbed him like a wrestler and thrown him down into the mud (v. 19). God has attacked him ruthlessly with his hands (v. 21). God has blown him around like a leaf in the wind (v. 22). And further, God refuses to talk to him or answer his cries for help (v. 20). God only seems to be interested in tormenting Job as much as possible before sending him to Sheol (v. 23).

Job's reaction to all of this was to put on sackcloth and weep (16:15-16). What could he possibly do to defend himself against such an angry God?

This raises a serious issue about God's nature that has turned some people away from God. The issue is this: Is your God loving or oppressive? How have you experienced him?

There is no question that steadfast, faithful love is the predominant characteristic of God in both Testaments (Deut. 7:7-9, 12-13; Hos. 3:1; 11:1-4; John 3:16; 1 John 4:7-12). The rescue from Egypt, the establishing of a covenant at Mount Sinai, the return of the exiles from Babylon, and the sending of God's Son, Jesus, are a few examples. But there are also plenty of examples of God's anger and violence against individu-

IV. Job 4-27: Job's Responses to His Friends

als, cities, and nations. Saul, Jezebel and Ahab, Sodom and Gomorrah, Egypt, Israel, Judah, and the people of Noah's day—all experienced God as violent at some point. In the book of Job, anger is associated with God eleven times (4:9; 9:5, 13; 14:13; 16:9; 19:11; 20:23, 28; 21:17; 35:15; 42:7). This is troubling. Is God truly violent and oppressive toward his creation? If so, when, how often, and are there any limitations?

Scholars have debated this topic for centuries, using Scripture, personal experiences, and theological reasoning. So our questions about it now are not new. The debate is still not settled, but most of us would at least like some clarity about what the issues are. The topic generally boils down to two questions. First, is biblical language about God's anger/wrath/violence only metaphorical, or does it express a reality about God's character? Second, if violence is truly a part of God's character, is it "a permanent attribute of God co-equal with love, or something more transient that is precipitated by man's [sinful] behavior?" (Herion 1992, 990).

With regard to the first question, both possibilities are supported in the book of Job. Job is a story told primarily in poetry. Poets often resort to metaphor and hyperbole to portray the deepest human feelings. Although Job's pain and losses were certainly real, these descriptions of God cannot be taken literally. God is not a lion, an archer, or a wrestler. Job's accusations in 16:7-14 of God's violent actions against him are what Job *felt* God was doing to him. Nowhere in the book does the author ever say that God was angry at Job or wanted to treat him violently.

At the same time, the events in the prologue reveal that God did allow the Examiner to treat Job violently, and God did admit that he was responsible for this (2:3). Job believed that God's wrath had been poured out on him, so much so that he wished he had never been born (ch. 3). Using all the information available to him, Job believed God was angry at him, and so did the three friends. They believed this because they had seen God punish wicked people prior to this. Consequently, they assumed that Job was getting the same kind of punishment. Further, the wisdom theology had supported this concept for generations, and biblical books such as Proverbs supported it as well. "People reap what they sow" was a hard and fast principle that was embedded in their culture (see 4:8; Prov. 22:8; Hos. 10:13; Gal. 6:7). Thus the Wisdom Literature, of which Job is a part, seems to support the idea that anger/wrath/violence are at least a small part of God's nature.

IV. Job 4-27: Job's Responses to His Friends

With regard to the second question, the occasions in the OT when God was provoked to anger and carried out his anger in violent ways were always related to sinful behavior (other than in Job). The destruction of human life in the time of Noah is the most obvious example (Gen. 6:5-7), but many other incidents are recorded, especially concerning the nation of Israel. During the period of the monarchy, the prophets repeatedly warned of the dangers associated with apostasy and disobedience to the covenant. And just as they predicted, God brought about the fall of Samaria and Jerusalem. The pain and misery experienced by the people were horrendous (Lam. 1–5). The writer of Lamentations attributes all of their suffering to God's anger at their sinfulness (1:14-15, 17-18; 2:1-8, 17, 22; 3:1-16, 41-45; 4:11, 16). Deliberate violations of the covenant always grieved God in the OT. And sinful behavior today grieves God just as much as it did in the days of the Israelites.

Further, there are numerous references in the OT that picture God as a military warrior, fighting sinful nations on behalf of his people (e.g., Exod. 15:1-18). At first, these nations were always Gentile, but by the time of the monarchy, God was angry at both Israel and Judah for their sinfulness. And Isaiah expanded the concept to include even all the peoples of the earth as the recipients of God's wrath (Isa. 24:1-13, 17-23). Therefore, human sin seems to be the catalyst that prods God into action in a violent way. At all other times, God's steadfast, faithful love seems to be the overriding characteristic of his nature.

One thing to keep in mind is that the picture of God in the Bible is very complex. There are multiple facets to his character that need to be taken into account (e.g., → the sermons below on Elihu, pp. 121-34). He is a God of both love and holiness. He acts as both a parent and a judge. He is the Creator as well as our Savior. He is both all-powerful and all-wise. And according to the book of Job (and the book of Revelation in the NT), one has to make a place for divine anger/wrath/violence in God's character on some occasions. Whether we as finite human beings can ever grasp the depths of his entire nature is questionable.

Before leaving these two chapters, let's return to the topic of human feelings. Job *felt* God was acting in violent ways toward him. And so he should have. Horrendous losses always produce intense feelings of pain. There is no question that Job suffered extreme losses in a short time—possessions, family, and health. How he kept any sanity is amazing. Only a person of outstanding integrity and loyalty to God could survive such

IV. Job 4-27: Job's Responses to His Friends

an onslaught. So we need to allow Job some space to vent his feelings. His cries give us a better understanding of how deeply his pain had affected him. The author did not intend for the reader to criticize Job's emotional outbursts. Rather, he was seeking empathy for the story's main character.

Sometimes God's people create false guilt for themselves over intense feelings that are perfectly normal. Who would not feel tremendous anguish over the loss of ten children? At the same time, other people react much differently because of their personality. Some may feel totally numb. This situation may also create false guilt over a lack of feelings. Job desperately needed friends to act as a sounding board so he could ventilate his feelings without reproach. And he needed an adequate amount of time for his emotions to heal. Unfortunately, his friends never recognized his needs, for they were too absorbed in their own agendas.

It is very reassuring to know that God never rejected Job's intense criticisms and extreme emotional language. Even when Job accused God of unjustly destroying both the blameless and the wicked (Job 9:22); of mocking the innocent (v. 23); of blindfolding judges (v. 24); of causing droughts and floods (12:15); of confusing and overthrowing rulers, priests, high officials, and nations (vv. 17-28); and of crushing Job himself (16:7-14), God accepted it all without comment. God did reprimand Job for some of the conclusions Job reached about God's supposed lack of justice (40:8), but he never tried to silence Job's feelings. God knows better than we do how our personalities are constructed. And he should, for he made us. Allowing Job to ventilate without reproach was one of God's gifts to Job that facilitated his healing.

Finally, people experience God in a variety of ways. There is no one universal feeling that all humans must experience every day in their relationship with God. "In some circumstances, God's presence *feels* violently oppressive. At other times, God's presence *feels* like the love of a mother" (Newsom 1996, 465). As each of us walks along the way of life, our age, our gender, our culture, our circumstances in life, and even our mood may influence how we perceive God. And these perceptions on any particular day may even change from hour to hour. Job's feelings about God in chapters 16–17 were certainly much different than those in 1:1-5 and 42:10-17.

People who are struggling with intense or wildly fluctuating emotional feelings about God may need some professional help to discover

IV. Job 4-27: Job's Responses to His Friends

their overall personality type and to determine what feelings are healthy and which ones are self-destructive. Unfortunately, Job had no expert in psychology or decent support system of friends to help him sort out his feelings. He had to live for many days with terrible emotions and without even a word from God. No wonder bitterness and fear took over his life. No wonder he regarded God as violent.

Possible Sermon Titles: "God as Enemy," "Is God Really Violent at Times?" "What Is Your Image of God: Loving or Oppressive?"

V. SUMMARY OF THE DIALOGUES

Three Blind Mice

Before leaving the dialogues between Job and his friends, your congregation may appreciate a short synopsis of the friends' best arguments and an evaluation of their effectiveness. Some general comments on Job's viewpoint would also be appropriate.

My commentary discusses eight points that the friends made in their speeches (see Bowes 2018, 300-301). These can be developed in greater detail as needed.

1. "Things do not happen without a reason."
2. "God has created an ordered world in which justice always prevails."
3. "God is a mysterious and transcendent being whose knowledge and power are far greater than ours."
4. "All humanity is imperfect. Only God is perfect."
5. "God is not the cause of humanity's troubles. We are."
6. "The best course of action in times of trouble is: commit your life to God and be patient."
7. "There can be value in suffering."
8. "If you have done something wrong, repent!"

Most of these arguments are generally true, and many people today still think about suffering in the same terms. But the arguments do not apply to Job's situation because the friends were unaware of the divine conversation in the prologue. As a result, their ignorance of all the facts renders their reasoning inapplicable and ineffective. They were three sincere, but blind mice.

The friends were also generally correct about the following:

1. They were correct that God treats us better than we deserve (Job 11:6). No one has ever earned the kind of unconditional love that God bestows on all humanity. However, the friends were insensitive and cruel to bring this up in their attempts to change Job's beliefs.
2. They were correct that *seeking God* is the best course of action in times of trouble. In fact, it is the best course of action at any time.
3. They were correct that God sometimes disciplines the righteous. He does so out of love and for their betterment (Prov. 3:11-12; 1 Cor. 11:32; Heb. 12:4-11). God's discipline is focused on our improvement, not his justice or retribution (→ the sermon below, "God as Disciplinarian," p. 133).

However, the friends were wrong in believing that God *always* rewards the righteous and *always* punishes the wicked. This is a good principle in general, but not one that can be universalized to all situations. For reasons known only to him, sometimes God causes/allows righteous people to suffer and the wicked to escape judgment in this life.

The friends can also teach us to put our opinions on hold until we have gathered all the facts. There are real dangers in prejudging people based on limited or superficial evidence. Further, the friends illustrate the impossibility of placing God in a box for us to analyze and explain. Divine mysteries will always abound.

Likewise, Job erred in trying to universalize the good life of the wicked (Job 21:6-16). Some wicked people do escape punishment in this life, but not all. And his claim that God had been unjust to him was faulty (19:6). He, too, was unaware of the divine conversation in the prologue and thus lacking all the evidence.

The one positive thing we can say about Job is that his attention was focused in the right direction. He did engage his friends in debate, hoping they could shed some light on his predicament. But once he recognized that they had their own agendas, he stated clearly that the real debate was between himself and God (13:1-3). Only God could explain the real reason for his troubles and the steps he needed to take to gain restoration. Except for the fact that the friends did provide a sounding board for Job's ideas, their advice was worthless (vv. 4-5).

V. Summary of the Dialogues

In the contest between the friends and Job, much more is at stake than simply the honor of winning an argument (Balentine 2006, 304). The whole nature of God, the nature of humanity, and the nature of the cosmos are brought into question. One's entire worldview is being debated. If the friends are correct, God is a person who operates according to rigid principles that demand total justice for every moral deed—whether good or bad. Human beings experience God primarily as judge. They can count on a blessed future by living a life pleasing to God. And each person's level of morality is plainly evident by the amount of suffering they have experienced in life.

The world of the friends' theology is one that many people prefer. It is predictable and comes with observable rewards. It is supported by *deductive* lines of reasoning that protect the nature of God at all costs. But it lasts only as long as one can avoid natural disasters, disease, and mistreatment from others. Then this worldview collapses. It can only be maintained thereafter at the price of one's honesty and by engaging in all kinds of mental gymnastics.

If Job is correct, God is not just. He operates however he wishes, sometimes rewarding the wicked and punishing the righteous and sometimes vice versa, for no good reason. Human beings cannot predict how God will treat them. Thus they live in an uncertain world, fearful of the future. Suffering does not mean a person has sinned. It simply indicates that God does not like you.

Job's world is shrouded in confusion rather than certainty. By the use of *inductive* reasoning, he arrives at the conclusion that justice is not a major concern to God. Too many good people experience severe suffering directly caused by God and without adequate explanation. God cannot be trusted to use his awesome power and knowledge in ways that will benefit humanity. One is left with a diminished view of God that fails to encourage true worship and service.

In a nutshell, both worldviews were lacking. Both needed a better understanding of God and his relationship with his creation. He is not rigid, but neither is he temperamental. He deeply desires fellowship with humanity and does everything possible to enable us to respond to his love and grace. He generally operates in ways that human beings would consider just, righteous, loving, faithful, and holy, but sometimes he makes exceptions that leave us baffled. These mysteries about God's decisions and actions can lead to confusion and even bitterness, as in

V. Summary of the Dialogues

Job's case. The loss of Job's wealth, health, and children was an experience for which he was not prepared. As a result, his bitterness should not surprise us.

However, humans need to remember that God is God. No one can force him to reveal his secrets or to act in ways contrary to his plans. Humans also need to accept that many unpleasant experiences in life are not caused by God at all. The world in which God has placed us is physically unstable in nature (illustrated by earthquakes, volcanoes, floods, and hurricanes) and morally stained by sin (illustrated by wars, crime, cruel and inhumane treatment of other human beings, and internet slander and bullying). Both Job and his friends never acknowledged this, and so their understanding of the causes of suffering and a proper reaction to it was deeply flawed.

Times of trouble should be viewed as opportunities to strengthen one's trust in God. Certainly the best way to react to life's tragedies is the one Job arrived at in the end (42:1-6). He finally acknowledged God's correct governance of the world, submitted himself to God's will, accepted God's mysteries, and continued living the righteous life he was living before the calamities struck. But before Job arrived at this position, he first needed to hear directly from God. And the same is true for each of us. Only a personal encounter with God can put our hearts and minds at ease when tragedy strikes.

Possible Sermon Titles: "Three Blind Mice," "The Mysteries of God," "Lessons from the Dialogues"

VI. JOB 28: INTERLUDE

The Way to Wisdom (Job 28)

There has been much discussion about the author of chapter 28 because this passage is so different from the rest of the book. My position is that it was written by the same author as the rest of the book. The author may have composed this chapter at an earlier time as a separate essay and then placed it here because it fit his literary purpose. Or he may have written it especially for this position.

For preaching purposes, introduce this passage as a short interlude that the author placed here to relieve the tension that had built up throughout the dialogues (see Bowes 2018, 303-4). It is calmly worded and reveals the author's viewpoint about the nature of wisdom and its relationship to God.

Once the tension in the story has dissipated in chapter 28, the author moves on to new speeches that rebuild the tension and move toward a climax. First, Job delivers a long, passionate defense of his righteousness (chs. 29–31). Then, a new, young man named Elihu enters the story (chs. 32–37). He angrily lashes out at everyone but offers few new ideas. Finally, God appears and thunders a magnificent speech from the heavens (chs. 38–41). Everyone is left speechless. Job mumbles a few words of apology, and then the book concludes with a prose epilogue.

Chapter 28 divides into three sections.

1. Human Beings Are Extremely Skilled in Advancing Knowledge about the Natural World and Using That Knowledge to Improve Their Lives (Job 28:1-11)

The first section praises the skills of human beings in finding and extracting precious minerals and gems from beneath the ground. The author

VI. Job 28: Interlude

seems very knowledgeable about the process of mining. This probably indicates he had actually visited a mine at some time in his life. He notes how mines were often located far from cities in mountainous terrain or desert regions. There the miners dug deep shafts into the ground or into the sides of mountains. When they found a vein of ore, they followed it until it ran out. The minerals and gems were chiseled out of the vein and hauled to the surface using ropes and baskets. No one above ground knew what the miners were doing below the surface. Even the keenest-eyed animals and birds were unaware of the miners' activities.

Mining was hard, dangerous work that took the lives of many of the miners. But most nations eagerly desired the products that came out of the ground. And so the miners toiled day after day in miserable conditions far from their families. Probably most of them were slaves or prisoners of war.

The author mentions the four most sought-after metals at that time—"silver," "gold," "iron," and "copper" (28:1-2). These metals provided many valuable products, such as tools, weapons, jewelry, and religious objects. One of the gems mentioned is "lapis lazuli" (v. 6). Lapis is a beautiful, royal-blue stone mined in Afghanistan. Merchants carried this stone as far away as Egypt because there was such a great demand for it.

At first glance, the first section appears to be simply a very knowledgeable description of one of the important industries in the ancient world. But the author is using this section to praise the skills and ingenuity of human beings. Seemingly there is nothing humans cannot accomplish when they set their minds to it.

This attitude is still prominent today, and there is evidence to support it. Think of all the accomplishments and discoveries by human beings in the areas of space, medicine, commerce, communication, and transportation during the last century. Human beings are fantastically inquisitive and creative.

2. Humans Are Total Failures in Finding Wisdom Because It Is Not a Natural Part of Our World That Can Be Extracted and Refined as One Does with Minerals (Job 28:12-19)

The author uses the first section to establish the background for the question he will ask in the second: How have humans fared in their search for "wisdom" (v. 12)? Wisdom is extremely valuable in accomplishing anything in life. In fact, it is more valuable than "gold," "silver,"

VI. Job 28: Interlude

"onyx," and "lapis lazuli," and so forth—some of the most precious minerals and gems known in the ancient world (vv. 15-19). Everyone wants wisdom and lots of it, because wisdom will enable people to make good decisions, thus improving their overall happiness and well-being. With all of their skills in finding hidden things under the ground and then turning them into useful products, shouldn't humans be able to discover wisdom just as they mine for silver?

Alas, humanity does not know how to find wisdom because its source is not "found in the land of the living" (v. 13). Even "the deep" and "the sea" (v. 14) that have existed since creation (Gen. 1:2) do not know where to find wisdom.

We would have to agree with the ancient author of Job. In spite of incredible advances in human knowledge since the time of Job, why are there still wars, crime, terrorists, poverty, greed, and dysfunctional families? Shouldn't we have figured out how to solve these problems by now?

It is not for lack of trying. Like miners in search of gold and silver, numerous people have made serious efforts to solve humanity's major problems. They have conducted years of research, interviewed thousands of people, written books, taught seminars, and invested millions of dollars. And some have even claimed to have found the answer. But no human being has ever discovered where and how to find wisdom *in this world*. And none ever will. The ancient writer of Ecclesiastes pointed this out centuries ago (Eccles. 8:16-17). Those who claim to be wise in these matters are only fooling themselves.

3. Only God Knows How to Find Wisdom and Use It (Job 28:20-28)

In the third section, the author notes the reason why humans are so ignorant: only God knows the way to find wisdom (28:23). There are several reasons for this.

First, God is the Creator (vv. 25-26). Since he brought everything into existence and ordered it according to his plans, he has an intimate knowledge of everything in the universe. Only he knows the purpose of every part of his universe and how it is supposed to operate.

Second, God is not localized to one place on earth like humans (v. 24). He sees the big picture as well as all the little details. He is constantly aware of everything going on "under the heavens" (v. 24).

Third, God made a thorough evaluation of wisdom even before he began his creative activity (v. 27). And he liked what he saw. Wisdom

VI. Job 28: Interlude

was so valuable that he appropriated it and used it to guide him as he brought the world into being (Prov. 8:22-31).

Consequently, in the author's mind, humans may have some small bit of knowledge about various aspects of the world, but only God has the wisdom to understand how it all fits together. The implication is that humans could live much better lives if they had the wisdom God has because then they could see the overall plan God has for the world and know where they fit in.

There is good news in the last verse in chapter 28. There we discover for the first time that God is willing to share his wisdom with the "human race" (v. 28). He does not wish to keep it for himself alone. He does not delight in seeing humans wander through life in ignorance and confusion. He desires that all human beings would find wisdom and appropriate it into their own lives.

With this offer of "wisdom" and "understanding" comes a prerequisite. One must fear God and turn away from evil (v. 28). In other words, true wisdom can be attained only by establishing a relationship with God. Without that relationship, all other human attempts to gain wisdom are doomed to failure.

One interesting way of looking at chapter 28 is to note how it provides an analogy with the debate that has raged throughout the dialogues (chs. 4–27). Job and his friends are like the miners of chapter 28. They have feverishly mined the world of knowledge looking for a correct understanding of Job's suffering. They have figuratively turned over every stone and looked under every rock. And they have drawn upon every resource of which they are aware—tradition, cause-and-effect reasoning, personal experiences, observations of the natural world, and even a divine visitation.

They have found a few precious minerals and gems in the process. For example, they have noted that God sometimes causes suffering as a means of discipline. And they have affirmed that we should seek God first whenever we run into trouble. But they have also mined many worthless, unusable rocks, such as the claim that Job is a sinner and is being punished by God.

The author then concludes his essay in chapter 28 by implying that just as the miners failed in their efforts to find wisdom, so Job and his friends have failed to unlock the mystery of Job's troubles. And they will always remain ignorant because only God knows the real reason why Job

VI. Job 28: Interlude

is suffering. The wisdom about some things in life will always remain a mystery to everyone except God.

This sermon could end with a challenge to examine one's own life in the light of verse 28. Does your life bear any evidence of being lived according to the wisdom that only God can provide? Or is it being directed by human advice, whether provided by yourself or others? True wisdom can only be gained through reverence and worship of God and submission to his will.

Possible Sermon Titles: "The Way to Wisdom," "True Wisdom: What Is Its Source?" "How Can One Gain True Wisdom?" "The Fear of the Lord—That Is Wisdom," "Gold or Wisdom? Which Is of More Value to You?" "Skilled in Going to the Moon, but a Failure in Finding Wisdom"

VII. JOB 29-31: JOB'S MANIFESTO

All of us are familiar with before-and-after pictures that reveal the results of a major change in one's life. For example, the before-and-after view of a house remodel, a major weight loss, a change in hairstyle, or the addition of braces to one's teeth. Chapters 29–30 provide a before-and-after summary of Job's life up to this point. The first picture (ch. 29) is of the blessed life he enjoyed prior to experiencing the Examiner's attacks. The second (ch. 30) is of the suffering and bitterness that now overwhelm him. When placed side by side, these two chapters are shocking. They speak to us of how quickly and drastically life can change.

Before the Calamities, I Was Living a Fantastic Life (Job 29)

The description Job gives of his earlier life is filled with superlatives. He mentions the following points.

1. God Was Blessing Him Abundantly (Job 29:1-6, 14)

Job had a large, happy family. His farms and businesses were doing extremely well. He felt secure from the troubles of life—both human made and nature caused. Righteousness and justice were such a natural part of his life that they seemed like articles of clothing (v. 14). And God was his ever-present friend who blessed him abundantly.

2. He Had Earned Tremendous Respect from His Community (Job 29:7-17)

Job's description of people's reactions when he went out in public is indicative of the amount of respect he received from others. Apparently, he had an assigned seat at the gate of his city among the elders. People stopped what they were doing when he showed up. Everyone wanted to know what he had to say.

However, what Job said was not nearly as important as what he did. Job had used his great wealth to benefit those who were needy in his society—"the poor," "the fatherless," "the one who was dying," "the widow," "the blind," "the lame," "the needy," and "the stranger" (vv. 12-13, 15-16). He had earned the praise of these people through his gifts and through his support of them in their times of need. He thoroughly enjoyed this ministry.

3. He Was Extremely Pleased with His Life (Job 29:18-20)

Job had nothing to complain about. Things were going well for him. He fully expected to live a long life surrounded by his family.

4. As a Leader of His Community, He Was Able to Provide Wise Counsel (Job 29:21-25)

The people of Uz regarded Job as a wise leader. They eagerly listened to his advice and followed his recommendations.

Most people would be quite envious of Job's earlier life. He seemingly was without a problem. And most of all, he was in an intimate relationship with God. He was truly a supersaint. No wonder he longed for those days again (vv. 1-6).

After the Calamities, I Wanted to Die (Job 30)

When you look back at history, some remarkable dividing points jump out at you. The most noticeable was the change from BC to AD. People living at that time did not know a major change was just beginning. They just went about their normal activities. But Jesus's coming to earth radically affected the course of events thereafter. Other major shifts in history include the conquests of Alexander the Great in the fourth century BC and the Reformation in the sixteenth century AD.

VII. Job 29-31: Job's Manifesto

Job, too, had a radical change in his life. That is what this book is about. Chapters 1 and 2 describe the tremendous reversal in his fortunes. Chapter 3 sums up his anguish immediately following the calamities. By the time we get to chapter 30, Job has had ample time to reflect on these catastrophes and how they have affected him. This chapter summarizes his feelings about his new life. It was like going from light to darkness, from good to evil, from blessing to punishment, from heaven to hell on earth (v. 26).

Job begins chapter 30 by noting again how the community of Uz had turned against him (see also 19:13-22). Once he lost his wealth, his health, and his ten children, he was no longer the respected leader looked up to by his community. In fact, they were afraid to be around him. They mocked him from a distance (30:1, 10). His name was now a "byword" for what happens to people when they reject God and turn to a life of sin (v. 9). Even the lowest classes of society derided him. Some of the crueler ones ventured close enough to "spit" in his face (v. 10). He compares his feelings about these social attacks to those of a city under siege (vv. 12-15) or an outcast driven away into the desert (v. 29).

The worst part of all this was that God had caused it to happen (v. 11). God seemed like a tyrant bent on driving Job to an early death. God was cruel, ruthless, and physically violent to Job (vv. 18-23). Further, God had refused to communicate with him about the reason for his actions (v. 20). In spite of repeated cries for help (vv. 20, 24), God had left Job alone in his misery.

What are we to make of these hard-hitting criticisms of God? Are they a fair evaluation of God's interactions with human beings? And do they represent the feelings of many people in the world today? Or was Job just an abnormal complainer/whiner? Have you yourself ever had these feelings toward God?

In answer to these questions, we need to remember that times of trouble sometimes bring out the worst in people. Scripture contains some wonderful promises that have lifted the spirits of God's people for centuries (e.g., Josh. 1:5, 9; Ps. 23; Isa. 40:28-31; John 14:27; Phil. 4:6-7, 19). These words have even been found on the lips of martyrs as they went to their executions. But not everyone is helped by them. Some refuse to believe that God cares about them. Some have been hit with so many crises and reversals in life that they feel as if they are under siege. They are reluctant even to get up in the morning lest another evil befall them.

VII. Job 29-31: Job's Manifesto

In such situations, God is an easy target to blame. After all, he created the world and ordered it, so he is ultimately responsible for what happens. And further, he is omniscient, so he sees all the activities of human beings. He should know when evil is about to take place. And he should also be able to prevent it, because he is omnipotent.

That line of reasoning has plagued humanity since the beginning of time, for we all want someone to blame when things go wrong. It somehow makes us feel better to be able to direct our anger at someone else and shout loud curses at that one. Just witness the insane tirades that break out on the internet after every crisis. People have their favorite targets—politicians, government officials, the media, large corporations, church leaders, and so forth—but inevitably it all comes back to God for creating such a world.

One of the lessons the book of Job teaches us is that this world's troubles originate in a variety of ways. Some come from God, some from nature, some are caused by other people, and some are self-caused. When people fail to recognize this and lash out at God, they reveal their own ignorance about the causes of suffering.

Another concept the book of Job teaches us is that we may never know the cause of some of our suffering. And it is fruitless to speculate and harmful to our spirit and our relationships with other people when we blame someone without knowing all the evidence. This is the chief criticism of the three friends. They blamed Job himself for all his problems. If they had known about the divine conversation between God and the Examiner, they never would have made that mistake.

We all would like to know the causes of all that happens to us in life, but unfortunately many events remain a mystery. Those who cannot live with mystery in their lives end up in constant bitterness and whining.

A third lesson is the fallacy of holding to a rigid cause-and-effect line of reasoning (see "Cause-and-Effect Reasoning" in Bowes 2018, 101-3). The three friends believed that one's fortunes in life were directly determined by one's righteousness or sinfulness. Righteousness always resulted in a good life, while sinfulness produced pain and suffering. Job agreed with them on this point, at least in theory, for this is what he had been taught (Job 30:26). Therefore, his outstanding righteousness should have given him the most blessed life on earth. And it did, for a while. But then the calamities struck. He had no explanation for their cause. Where were the rewards he had enjoyed earlier? Had he sinned,

VII. Job 29-31: Job's Manifesto

as the friends suggested? He was adamant that he had not. So what had caused his sudden change in fortune? Job pleaded with God for an answer. God's silence only made him more desperate and bitter.

Job had fallen into the same trap as those who today believe in the gospel of success (the prosperity gospel). These people live righteous lives expecting a reward. Sometimes life treats them well, and they see this as confirmation of their beliefs. But when things go badly, they have no explanation. When cancer strikes or a tornado knocks down their house or a child turns to drugs, they are just as mystified as Job. They can only retreat into themselves, taking their spiritual pulse and trying to identify a sinful thought or action that may signal God's displeasure.

Many of us can probably identify at least one major defining moment in our lives when everything changed. Maybe a parent died at an early age. Maybe there was a bitter divorce in the family. Maybe a natural disaster destroyed our home. Or maybe our job disappeared during an economic recession. Looking back on it, we can see definite changes that resulted from that experience.

Hopefully, people learn something from their calamities that make them better individuals—but maybe not. Nothing in the book up to this point indicates that Job had made any positive steps toward an emotional recovery from his dreadful experiences. He was still focused on the past—blaming God for causing these events and bitter that God had not spoken to him about them. That's a choice he made, and some people have followed him along the same path.

However, there is a much better approach available to each of us. Turning one's life over to God and letting go of life's problems is the most invigorating and refreshing experience available to human beings. In contrast to Job, it is like going from evil to good, from darkness to light (30:26). For people growing up in a Christian home, the divine reversal that results may not be that radical. But for others in deep sin, it is the most life-changing experience that ever happened to them.

When preaching from this text, one could conclude with a personal testimony or some examples from other people's lives, such as John Wesley's Aldersgate experience.

Possible Sermon Titles: "Before and After," "Defining Moments in Life," "Turning Points in Life," "Life-changing Experiences," "But Now They Mock Me," "My Lyre Is Turned to Mourning," "When I Looked for Good, Evil Came"

VII. Job 29-31: Job's Manifesto

I Do Not Deserve All This Suffering (Job 31)

Probably the first passage that comes to mind when one thinks about Christian ethics is the Sermon on the Mount (Matt. 5–7). There Jesus laid out some of the core principles of Christianity, such as meekness, righteousness, mercy, peace, and love. But the OT was also concerned with ethics in everyday life. And Job 31 is one of the most important passages on this topic in all of the OT.

Back in chapter 3 Job had been very critical of God for allowing him to be born. He believed he could have avoided all of his problems if he had never existed. But since God had allowed him to be conceived, to be born, and to grow into adulthood, his next best option was to die right now. And that is what he desperately wanted to happen as soon as possible (6:8-9).

By the time we get to chapter 31, Job is no longer pleading for death. He does not need to because a quick glance at his body tells him that death is not far off. His disease had turned his skin "black" (30:30). He knows that Sheol is just around the corner (v. 31). However, before he dies, Job wants to give one last testimony of his innocence. Just in case anyone still does not believe him, he is going to describe in detail ten common sins he has scrupulously avoided. This should be proof enough that he is still worthy of being called a supersaint, as in chapter 1.

Job wants to show that the friends were completely wrong in their accusation that he is a sinner. The fact that they never respond to Job's testimony here is strong evidence they know he had bested them. Job also opens the door for God to step forward and present any evidence to the contrary. God should speak up now or else acknowledge that Job has been speaking the truth.

Job is so convinced he is correct about his innocence that he calls down four curses on himself if anyone can prove he is wrong. These are terrible curses that none in their right minds would ever wish on themselves if they had any doubt about their personal integrity. The curses include the loss of his crops (31:8), a sexual assault on his wife (v. 10), the loss of the mobility of his arm (v. 22), and the infertility of his land (v. 40). Job is so confident he is right that he is not afraid to make such curses. Job never experiences these curses, so God must agree that Job is innocent. The calling down of curses on oneself to declare one's innocence is a form that is found in other places in the OT. For example,

VII. Job 29-31: Job's Manifesto

in Psalm 7:3-5 [4-6 HB] the psalmist is so confident that he has never harmed his enemy that he tells God to let his enemy kill him if God can prove otherwise.

The ten sins Job believes he has avoided are as follows (you can provide more detail on each of these if so desired):
1. Lust (Job 31:1-4)
2. Dishonesty and straying from God (vv. 5-8)
3. Adultery (vv. 9-12)
4. Mistreatment of servants (vv. 13-15)
5. Lack of compassion for the needy (vv. 16-23)
6. Greed and idolatry (vv. 24-28)
7. Vindictiveness against an enemy (vv. 29-30)
8. Lack of hospitality for strangers (vv. 31-32)
9. Concealment of one's sins (vv. 33-34)
10. Exploitation of one's land and employees (vv. 38-40)

One immediately notices the wide range of sins. Certainly, this is not a comprehensive list, but it does indicate that Job was attempting to cover all bases. Over half of them deal with *outward* sinful relationships with other people: relationships in the home (nos. 3 and 4), relationships in one's business dealings (no. 10), relationships with those in society who have needs (nos. 5 and 8), and relationships with one's enemies (no. 7). These are the kinds of sins that the three friends or anyone else could easily have observed, and in fact Eliphaz tried to pin some of them on Job, but without success (22:4-11).

However, there are other sins in the list that no one else except Job and God would ever know. These are *inward* sins of the heart that most people keep concealed. They include lust (no. 1), dishonesty (no. 2), greed and idolatry (no. 6), and deceitfulness (no. 9). Job's oath of innocence concerning these sins and his request for God to curse him if found guilty are appropriate because only God would know if he had committed them.

If one is going to make things completely right with God, both inward and outward sins must be confessed and forgiven. This is a truth emphasized in other places in the OT: Exod. 20:2-17; Lev. 19; Deut. 5:6-21; 1 Sam. 15:22-23; Pss. 15; 19:12-14 [13-15 HB]; 24:3-4; 51; 139:23-24; Ezek. 18; 36:25-27.

In the book of Job, Eliphaz (4:17-19; 15:15-16), Zophar (11:4-6), and Bildad (25:4-6) deny that human beings can ever be cleansed of all sin.

Humans are always morally deficient. They base their argument on a view that emphasizes the totally inferior nature of humanity compared to God. Even angels are less than God in purity, so how can humans ever achieve a pure heart?

Job begs to differ. He believes that even though humans are inferior to God in many ways, God desires that they strive to be pure like him with their entire beings. His list in chapter 31 is meant to show that he knows exactly what God's requirements are. Both outer actions and inner thoughts must be cleansed and made holy so that nothing separates a person from God. Only then can they claim to be righteous (see also "The Interior Dimension of Holiness" in Bowes 2018, 329).

Job's conscience is now clear that he is "blameless and upright." Both the author and God have already confirmed that he is correct in this (1:1, 8; 2:3). Chapter 31 only expands on that evaluation by providing numerous examples of Job's spiritual life in action. This is his testimony of the kinds of things he has done or avoided to gain God's favor and maintain a right relationship with him. He does not know of anything else he could do to improve on this list.

Nevertheless, Job is deeply troubled that God does not acknowledge Job's righteousness and bless him again as he did in earlier times (ch. 29). This puzzlement leads Job to plead with God once more to explain the reason for his suffering (31:35-37). He is ready to defend his righteousness to God or to anyone else who questions his integrity. And if perchance God should be able to prove that Job has some hidden sin in his life, Job states that he is willing to wear a big signboard that spells out God's accusation so everyone can see that God is right and Job is wrong.

One good way to conclude this sermon would be to move to the NT and draw parallels with Jesus's call to holy living. Even a short passage such as the Beatitudes (Matt. 5:3-12) includes examples of both the inward nature of holy living and its outward manifestations. Thus God speaks through both Testaments concerning what it means for humans to be holy and pleasing to him.

Possible Sermon Titles: "Moral Standards in the Kingdom of God," "God Desires a Pure Heart," "Inward and Outward Righteousness," "I Am Innocent"

VIII. JOB 32-37: ELIHU

A Young Whippersnapper Takes on Job and His Friends (Job 32:1-5)

In political election years, what is your reaction after listening to a group of people debate the strengths and weaknesses of each candidate? It might be a desire to get into the debate and correct the views and prejudices that have been passionately argued. Such is the attitude of our next character.

In chapters 32–37, we are introduced to a new character by the name of Elihu. He and his speech are unique in several ways.

- He is the only major human character in the book to have a Hebrew name. He is not an Israelite, but his theology definitely is.
- He is never mentioned before or after these chapters. And none of the other characters ever discuss his main points. So we are completely on our own in evaluating the merits of his speech.
- There are some linguistic differences between Elihu's speech and the rest of the book. For example, Elihu mentions Job's name nine times, whereas the friends never use it.
- Some scholars have suggested that he is an intrusion into the story. At this point, the book should proceed to God's speeches, for it needs a climax to all of the tensions in the dialogues. These scholars even suggest that Elihu's speech was written much later by a different author. But the evidence for a second author is subjective and not sustainable (for more discussion, see Bowes 2018, 335-38).

VIII. Job 32-37: Elihu

Probably the best way to view Elihu is as an energetic, young man from Uz who has been lurking in the background, listening to the speeches of Job and his three friends. He is never called a friend. He is solely an outside observer who is trying to make sense of Job's situation and the comments he has heard in the dialogues (chs. 4–27). Therefore, it is easy for him to criticize, since there is no personal relationship that might hold him back from speaking his mind (32:17-22). He is also not a wise, old sage, like the three friends. He is not bound by the wisdom theology, although he holds to most of its views.

While listening to Job and his friends, Elihu became very angry (the author describes Elihu as "angry" four times in 32:1-5). But out of respect for the ages of the other speakers, he had remained silent. He was only in his late teens or twenties. He was very gifted in logical-reasoning and problem-solving skills, so he could see major mistakes in the arguments presented in the dialogues. But he knew he had best keep quiet while his elders were speaking.

As soon as Job and his friends ceased their debate, Elihu saw an opportunity to present his views. He jumped right into the debate and proceeded to criticize everyone who had spoken. Consequently, in Elihu, we have the reasoning of a young, outside observer with an Israelite way of thinking. By looking at Elihu's speech, preachers have a ready-made text to review some of the earlier discussions, pointing out strengths and weaknesses on each side of the debate.

According to the literary formulas in 32:6; 34:1; 35:1; and 36:1, Elihu seems to have four separate speeches. But in actuality, this is one long monologue that forms the longest speech in the book.

Elihu had one glaring fault that tends to turn readers against him. He was overly confident in his own ability to solve Job's problems. This egotistical attitude was probably related to his youth (32:6–33:7; 33:31-33; 36:1-4). Even though he was much younger than the other speakers, he claimed to have perfect knowledge about Job's situation (36:4). He tried to justify his views by claiming that God had spoken to him directly with the truth (32:8).

However, Elihu is not the only one in the book with a bad attitude. Each of the other human characters has some type of attitude problem as well. Bitterness is the issue that consumes Job and his wife. They feel terribly wronged by God, and bitterness is their response. The three friends display a lack of compassion for Job. Nowhere do they express

VIII. Job 32-37: Elihu

any empathy for his plight. In addition, their hasty conclusion that Job is a sinner reveals their proneness to prejudge. The one bad attitude that all the characters possess is arrogance. Each one thinks that their opinion is the correct one. No one is interested in really listening to the others' points of view.

Attitudes are an important consideration in the Christian life. They reflect what is going on in one's heart. Negative attitudes are especially damaging to the kingdom of God, hindering the work of God's Spirit and driving people away.

Elihu had three purposes in speaking. The first was to criticize the three friends for giving up the debate. Their silence indicated they had surrendered to the power of Job's arguments. Their frustration at Job's obstinacy probably contributed to their decision to quit. Elihu interpreted this as a weakness on their part. They were defeated. They had let Job best them in the debate. So Elihu scolded them for giving up. He stated that he intended to carry on the same line of reasoning the friends had pursued.

His second purpose was to criticize Job. Elihu had heard Job make a number of comments about himself and God that were just plain erroneous (34:5-9). For example, Job had insisted he was completely innocent of sin. Therefore, God was punishing him unjustly. Further, he had claimed that God would not even speak to him about why he was being punished. These assertions needed to be corrected before anyone accepted them as the truth. Just because Job had voiced them in a loud, belligerent voice did not make them true. In Elihu's thinking, Job was a rebel (v. 37). He was stating opinions that were false and guilty of dishonoring God.

A third purpose was to defend God's character. Elihu believed God's character had been besmirched in the dialogues. He was especially concerned with errors in Job's thinking about God's relationship to justice. Overall, Elihu's speech touches on a wide range of God's characteristics. This gives preachers an opportunity to present a broad understanding of the nature of God. This is what we will concentrate on in this chapter.

Each of Elihu's descriptions of God deserves an entire sermon, but of course there is not adequate time for such an endeavor. Consequently, preachers must make some decisions about what to use. Some points can be combined, and some can be omitted simply because they were covered in earlier sermons from the dialogues. One also needs to keep in

VIII. Job 32-37: Elihu

mind that the God speeches that follow (chs. 38–41) cover many of the same topics as Elihu's, so it may be more appropriate to wait until then.

Several sermon ideas on the nature of God are presented in the following pages. They are focused primarily on what Elihu says about them, but they can be supplemented with other passages from outside the book of Job.

Possible Sermon Titles: "One Who Has Perfect Knowledge Is with You," "Youth Desires to Speak," "The Younger Generation Has Something to Say," "An Angry Young Man with All the Answers," "Attitudes Matter"

God as Creator (Job 33:4, 6; 35:9-11; 37:2-13)

Any discussion about God always begins with creation. His founding of the world and ordering it according to his wisdom are foundational to all books in both Testaments. The book of Job especially emphasizes this concept (in addition to Elihu's speech, see 5:9-10; 9:1-13; 10:8; 11:7-9; 12:7-10, 13-25; 25:2-3; 26:5-14; 27:11-12; 28:20-28; plus, see God's speeches in chs. 38–41).

In these passages God is described as the one who stretched out the heavens and set the stars in their constellations. He created a whole host of strange-looking animals that bring him pleasure. He causes the rain to fall, the sun to rise, and the wind to blow. He sometimes sends natural disasters such as earthquakes and floods. And he is the source of eclipses of the sun and moon. These are all a part of God's order.

God is also the "Maker" of humanity (33:4, 6; 35:9-11). He accomplished this by forming human beings out of the clay and breathing into them his breath (also Gen. 2:7).

In Job 37:2-13, Elihu praises God's control of nature through his mighty power. Especially important is verse 13. Here he gives three reasons for God's actions in the world. The first is literally "for the rod" (AT), which the NRSV interprets as "for correction." Based on the usage of this word in other places, the word "rod" symbolizes *punishment* for the wicked, *discipline* for those who have neglected God, and *authority* over all creatures in the entire universe. God's authority deserves our awe and respect. This reason for God's actions implies that we live in a moral universe, where choices are made for good or for bad. Sometimes God sees a need to use his rod in situations where bad choices have been made.

The second reason for God's actions is "for his land" (NRSV). The land is in need of water, nutrients, and the sun in order to provide food for humanity and the animal kingdom. God provides just exactly what the land needs to meet our nutritional needs. Deserts are places where God has withheld his rain from the land.

The third reason for God's actions is "for love" (NRSV). Whereas the first two reasons emphasize God's actions in response to needs in either humanity or nature, the third focuses on God's desire to act in ways not required. God is not obligated to love. He chooses to do so.

The word "love" (*ḥesed*; sometimes translated "steadfast love," "unfailing love," "loving-kindness," "mercy," etc.) is normally used in the OT in reference to God's faithful relationship to his people Israel. God entered into a covenant with Israel at Mount Sinai, and he is fully committed to providing for their welfare and protection. He desires the best for them. And he promises to bless them when they are obedient. The incarnation is an example of God's *ḥesed* in the NT (John 3:16).

However, Elihu uses the term "love" to describe God's steadfast commitment to caring for his entire creation, not just Israel. A good example of the kind of divine love that Elihu has in mind is God's covenant with all living creatures following the flood (Gen. 9:8-17). There God promised never again to destroy all life.

Possible Sermon Titles: "Three Reasons for God's Actions," "I, Too, Am a Piece of Clay"

God as Sovereign (Job 33:12; 34:13-15, 21-28; 36:5, 22-33; 37:1-24)

God's sovereignty and omnipotence are two complementary characteristics. The first speaks of his control over every aspect of life. Both individuals (33:12) and nations (36:31) are bound by the limitations God imposes on them. The NT indicates that even Satan and the forces of evil are limited by God's governance of the world (Rom. 16:20; Rev. 20:1-10). But God's sovereignty should not frighten us, for without his interest in governing the world and caring for its needs we all would perish (Job 34:14-15).

Elihu's rhetorical questions in 34:13 are intended to raise the issue of who is actually in charge of life. Does God's sovereignty derive from someone higher than himself who appointed him to exercise governance

VIII. Job 32-37: Elihu

of the world? Elihu's answer is no. God's acts of creation make him the sole ruler of his creation and entitle him to govern as he sees fit. He is not limited by anyone else.

Another characteristic of God is omnipotence—the attribute that enables him to exercise sovereignty. Elihu speaks eloquently of God's use of his power through nature (36:22–37:24). His deeds are tremendously powerful and "beyond our understanding" (36:26). Thunderstorms, lightning, and snow are just a few examples of God's mighty works.

God's sovereignty and omnipotence should call forth two human reactions. The first is praise (36:24)—that is, giving voice to one's recognition of God's greatness. The second is a desire to learn from the Master Teacher (v. 22). If humans want to be wise in their understanding of life and the nature of things, they need to choose a classroom where God is the professor. Both reactions require a humble acknowledgment that God's power and wisdom are far greater than that of human beings (v. 26).

Elihu believed that Job had rejected both of these reactions and turned to a life of "rebellion" (34:37). But just like the three friends, he failed to really listen to Job's heart. He allowed Job's appearance and arrogant attitude to influence his evaluation of Job's condition.

Even though God controls all of life through his sovereignty and omnipotence, there is still room for human freedom. He has self-limited himself to allow for human free will. Humans have the freedom to do whatever they wish. But Elihu knows it is foolish to throw off God's restraints and seek to rule a kingdom of one's own making. His last words are an attempt to shame Job against thinking this way (37:14-24). A comparison of Job's puny power with the might and majesty of the Almighty is laughable.

Possible Sermon Titles: "Don't Mess with God," "Can You Do What God Can Do?"

God as Just (Job 34:1-8, 10-30; 35:1-8; 36:3)

Elihu is especially critical of Job's remarks about God's lack of justice in ruling the world. In an earlier speech Job had accused God of injustice in regard to himself (27:2-6). God had repeatedly attacked him with one calamity after another in spite of Job being completely innocent of sin.

Job had also criticized God's treatment of the wicked (21:7-33). God blessed the wicked and caused them to prosper. They never suffered any of the calamities Job had experienced. Hence, for Job there was no reason to serve God because there was no benefit in doing so.

Job's complaints are still heard today. People note how the divide between the rich and the poor grows bigger every year, how the wealthy are able to influence the courts to avoid jail time, and how the powerful always seem to get their way. They rightfully ask, "Where is justice? Why does God not do anything?"

For Elihu, Job's position was unthinkable (34:12). Job was just plain wrong (v. 35). Elihu's rebuttal is as follows.

First, God always rewards the righteous and punishes the wicked (vv. 10-12). That is the reward system by which he operates. It is a part of his nature. Even kings and nobles experience God's wrath if they are sinful (vv. 16-30).

This is generally true. God does have a reward system that rewards righteousness and punishes wickedness. The Bible presents many examples that bear this out. Even the best of kings, such as David, experienced God's judgment for their sins. And the book of Revelation confirms that the wicked will receive God's final judgment at the end of time (20:11-15).

However, Job's question about why *he* was suffering is a valid one. Does God *always* reward the righteous and punish the wicked? The answer is no. God sometimes blesses people who do not deserve it. Zophar was right that God had already treated Job better than he deserved (Job 11:6). God does so because he loves us. For reasons of his own choosing, he sometimes surprises both the saint and the sinner with undeserved blessings. These are certainly outside the normal reward system. No one seems to complain about such gracious and merciful gifts.

At the same time, God sometimes allows suffering into the lives of people who are living righteously. The reasons for this are not always immediately apparent (see Gen. 45:5-7). And sometimes God does not reveal them at all. He remains silent (→ sermon below, "God as Free and Mysterious," p. 128).

It is also important to recognize that not all suffering is a punishment for sin. Suffering can occur for many other reasons that are not related to God's reward system (see "The Nature of Suffering" in Bowes 2018, 408-9). In Job's case, the prologue states that Job was not being punished at all. He was being tested on the reasons for his faith. So the issue of God's justice should not even apply. But of course, Elihu and the three friends were unaware of this. Even Job was confused about this matter.

In answer to Job's criticisms about God's justice, generally speaking God rewards the righteous and punishes the wicked, keeping in mind that rewards and punishments are not just material but can come in many forms. But the Bible is clear that exceptions to the general rule do occur. Our trust in him should remain constant no matter what may occur.

Second, God's standards of justice are ones *he* has established and chooses to adhere to. No one can force God to act in ways contrary to his nature (Job 34:5-9, 31-33). God sees the hearts of each individual and makes his evaluation accordingly. He cannot be fooled or bribed into making a wrong judgment.

Third, when Job denied that there was any benefit in serving God, he failed to consider how righteousness affects other people (35:1-8). Job's appraisal of the benefits of living righteously was too inwardly focused. He needed to enlarge his perspective to include the impact righteous people have on those in their circles of influence.

Abraham is a good example of a person whose faith was known not only by his immediate family but also by his clan in later generations and by millions of believers ever since. Jesus's words about being "salt" and "light" were intended to encourage righteous living so that one's social environment "may see your good deeds and glorify your Father in heaven" (Matt. 5:13-16).

(For further comments on the topic of God's justice, → the sermon above, "God Does Not Pervert Justice," p. 66, and the one below, "God's System of Justice," p. 138.)

Possible Sermon Titles: "It Is Unthinkable That God Would Pervert Justice," "Does God Pervert Justice?" "Does God Really Repay Everyone for What They Have Done?" "There Is No Profit in Trying to Please God"

God as Free and Mysterious (Job 34:29-30; 36:26, 29-30; 37:5-8)

Humanity has continually tried to place God in a box and restrict his ability to function in divine ways. As Murphy says, "Humans seem fundamentally unable to tolerate a God who is truly free. He must act

VIII. Job 32-37: Elihu

according to the definition laid down by them" (1977, 84). We want God to act in ways that fulfill our expectations. But if God did so, he would cease to be God. He would become a creature fashioned in the human image rather than the other way around (Gen. 1:26-27).

The three friends insisted that God *always* acted in predictable ways. His divine plans had been revealed to human beings, and thus they could depend on him always to conduct himself in these ways. They particularly applied this principle to the matter of divine justice and retribution, but other attributes of God were also held to be true in the same way.

Job had generally agreed with the three friends on this point up until he experienced his calamities. Then he parted ways with them. His own suffering had convinced him he was an exception to God's normal ways of acting. His heart was holy, and his behavior was righteous. But yet he suffered horrendous losses, and he did not know why.

Elihu's answer to Job focused on human finitude and ignorance. He insisted that God's ways are beyond the limits of human comprehension (Job 36:26). He was referring primarily to God's actions in creation and throughout nature. But God also involves himself in humanity's affairs as he sees fit. Sometimes he acts in bold ways, and other times he remains silent (34:29-30). His freedom to do either may create confusion and misunderstanding in the minds of his creatures. In thinking this way, Elihu was echoing Isaiah 55:9: "As the heavens are higher than the earth, so are my ways higher than your ways and my thoughts than your thoughts."

Elihu thinks Job is foolish to demand answers from God that God may not want to reveal. God has the right to remain silent. Job may never know what God is up to. Neither may we.

Thus God's power and freedom are the sources of the divine mysteries with which humans must live. As Paul said, we sometimes see life "in a mirror, dimly" (1 Cor. 13:12, NRSV). God usually acts in consistent ways that humans can count on, but sometimes he chooses differently. This does not mean he is capricious or unreliable. It simply means that he is too great to be confined inside the box of human expectations.

Balentine, following Richard Friedman (*The Disappearance of God: A Divine Mystery* [Boston: Little, Brown and Company, 1995]), takes God's mysteriousness a step further (2006, 377-79). He suggests that God "purposefully" hides himself from humanity "to encourage and promote a greater human responsibility for life on earth" (377). In other words, God's hiddenness is not just due to his freedom and his infinite nature, which is so far above human finitude. It is also intended to prod humanity into accepting its role in the governance of the world.

If God intervened in human activities every time something went wrong, there would be no role for humans to play. But in fact, God eagerly desires for humans to shoulder their part of the load of governance. That is what the psalmist meant when he said that God has given humanity "dominion" (Ps. 8:6 [7 HB], NRSV) over creation. God wants us to share his desires and values concerning such concepts as the worth of every human being, justice for every human being, compassion for the less fortunate, and protection of the earth. And he wants us to do something about them. He will help us when he sees fit, but he wants and expects us to take the initiative and strive for these values to be upheld and practiced. Humans are fully equipped to deal with most of the world's problems (Clines 2006, 617), but we would rather complain and blame God than roll up our sleeves and get to work.

Because God is free and mysterious, some of the deepest questions about life cannot be answered with a simple explanation or a strong yes or no. In fact, it may not be possible to answer them at all. That troubles some people who insist on a completely ordered world and short, black-and-white answers to all of life's questions. The book of Job helps us to realize that sometimes saying "I don't know" is more truthful than trying to justify possible options.

One good example of the effect of God's mysteriousness on human beings is the tortured attempt to find rational explanations for innocent suffering. Just like Job's friends, some people think they have a good answer for God's role in the death of so many people in the Haitian earthquake (2010) or the Indonesian tsunami (2004) or even in the ancient disaster at Pompey (79). But in fact, there simply is no good explanation for *why* some things happen at particular times.

Possible Sermon Titles: "Beyond Our Understanding," "Hurricanes, Cancer, and War: Why Does God Allow These Tragedies to Happen?" "What Is the Human Role in Governing the World?"

God as Communicator (Job 33:13-30; 36:8-12)

In the dialogue section (chs. 4–27), each of the three friends offered a word of hope to Job in their first speeches (5:17-26; 8:5-7, 20-22;

VIII. Job 32-37: Elihu

11:13-20). At that point, they believed that Job would heed their advice and submit his life to God. By the time of the second cycle of speeches, there was no word of hope. They had listened to Job's bitter complaints and decided it would be more appropriate to point out the terrible consequences of rejecting God. They were afraid he was on the verge of joining the wicked. His suffering was a sign that God was already starting to punish him. In the third cycle, Eliphaz offered again a tiny word of hope, but it was conditional on Job's repentance (22:21-30).

Elihu, too, wanted to offer Job some hope, but he takes a different approach. He had heard Job complain on several occasions about his lack of communication with God. Job knew from his earlier life that fellowship with God was one of the joys of those who serve him (29:4-6). But when the calamities struck, God had ceased to speak with him. Job was certain this was due to God's anger, but he did not know why God was angry at him.

God's sudden silence completely baffled Job. Unless God resumed talking again, Job knew there was no hope for him. Without any communication from God, Sheol/death seemed like a better option to him than life.

Elihu's approach to this problem was to point out God's continual interest in human beings (33:13-14). God never abandons us, no matter how far we drift away from him. He is the "Hound of Heaven" (see footnote on p. 65), who always seeks fellowship with all his creatures.

As Elihu saw it, the problem of communication that Job was experiencing was due to Job's lack of attentiveness rather than God's lack of desire. To prove this, Elihu drew Job's attention to three ways that God speaks to people—through dreams, through physical suffering, and through angels (33:13-30). Job had already testified to experiencing the first two, and the third he had longed for. So Elihu's point here is to clarify for Job God's methods of communication and thus open up his thinking to what God had been trying to say to him already.

According to Elihu, one method God uses to communicate with people is through dreams (vv. 15-18). Job had already indicated that he was having trouble sleeping at night because of terrible nightmares (7:13-14). He believed God was causing them.

Elihu picked up on this idea and pointed out that God was probably trying to speak to Job through these nightmares. Instead of passing them off as a form of divine harassment, Job should analyze his dreams and figure out what God was trying to say to him. Perhaps God was using Job's dreams to warn him of the dangers of sin and pride that lead toward Sheol.

One should not regard Elihu's point here as indicating that dreams always have some hidden message from God that we need to hear and act on. He is simply noting that God *can* use dreams if he wishes. We have a few examples in Scripture where God did use dreams to convey a needed message (Gen. 37:5-11; 40:1-23; 41:1-40; Matt. 1:18-25). The majority of our dreams are fairly innocent, and some may even be comical. Others may be nightmares like Job's. Psychologists have concluded that most dreams are simply one way our minds effectively process some of the activities that occur during the day.

Another method God uses to communicate is through sickness and physical suffering (Job 33:19-22). People may feel as if they are about to die, but God is not interested in killing them. He only wants to get their attention through chastening. His hope is that they will come to their senses and come back to him. Not all sickness can be attributed to God's chastening, but some may be. In Elihu's thinking, Job's terrible skin disease was a definite message from God that Job should take seriously as a warning about the way his life was headed.

Third, God tries to communicate with people through divine messengers—angels. These intermediaries act on God's behalf, delivering direct messages between God and individuals. In an earlier speech Job had requested the usage of such a person to mediate his dispute with God (9:33-34), but he never really believed such a person existed. Elihu firmly believed that these messengers do exist and that they could very well be speaking to God about Job right now. If that were the case, Job might be on the verge of complete reconciliation with God.

The point of this sermon is to help people think about ways God speaks to us today, as well as reasons why he may remain silent. Perhaps like Job, we have been missing God's attempts to communicate with us because of our inattentiveness caused by such things as busyness, apathy, carelessness, failing to order and prioritize our lives, and setting wrong goals in life.

If that is the case, now is the time to open up the channels of communication on our end. As Elihu notes, the problem of communication does not lie with God; it lies with us. God deeply desires to communicate with every person and will do so if we make ourselves available.

VIII. Job 32-37: Elihu

Possible Sermon Titles: "Can You Hear Me Now?" "How Does God Communicate with You?" "Is Your Cell Phone Dead?" "Oh, That God Would Speak to You," "If God Hides His Face, Who Can See Him?"

God as Disciplinarian (Job 36:5-15)

Back in 5:17-27, Eliphaz introduced the subject of God's discipline as a possible explanation for Job's suffering. There he noted that God sometimes disciplines us out of a desire to correct us or improve us. God plays the role of a good parent, observing when we are starting to drift away from him. He knows that his discipline will cause us temporary suffering, but in return he gets back a more mature, faithful servant. Eliphaz concluded that Job should welcome his present suffering as a sign that God was correcting him. If he accepted God's corrections and reformed his ways, his anguish would soon pass, and he would then enjoy a long, fruitful life.

In 36:5-15, Elihu emphasizes two additional points. First, from God's standpoint, there is a major difference between the truly wicked and the suffering righteous (v. 6). The former are evil. They mock God and his people and do whatever they can to oppose God's kingdom here on earth. The latter believe in God and want his will to be done. But they have drifted away from a close relationship with God for whatever reason and are in need of God's discipline.

The former are spiritually hopeless, although God would welcome them back if they changed their attitude. But as long as they continue their opposition to God, God is unable to help them. In Elihu's mind, they are headed for a tragic and early death (v. 12).

Elihu believes that Job is one of the latter—the suffering righteous. He has grieved God in some way and thus is being disciplined. Elihu is trying to warn Job against drifting into the camp of the wicked lest he experience God's awful judgment reserved for the truly evil.

This thought opens the door for preachers to comment on the various levels of morality in the world. Spirituality is not measured in only black and white. There are various shades of gray. People who move away from God usually do so in gradual stages, sometimes without even realizing how far they have drifted. God searches them out and sometimes uses the hard experiences of life to awaken them and draw them back to himself. No doubt, everyone reading this book can identify times in their lives when they have drifted away from God on the currents of life and been in need of his discipline. Thankfully, God has not deserted us on such occasions.

The second thought Elihu emphasizes is the importance of a right response when we are afflicted with suffering. One bad response is to accuse God of being unjust (vv. 17-18; see NRSV). We can always find wicked people who are well off and then accuse God of favoring them over us/the righteous. But such a response only gets us mired in self-pity rather than seeking hope.

A second bad response is to trust in one's own ability to extricate oneself from suffering. No human being is able to do so. Neither one's cries for help (incorrectly translated "wealth" in the NIV) nor one's mighty efforts can solve the problem of suffering in life (v. 19).

A third bad response is to try to escape this world through death/suicide (v. 20; see NRSV). That solves nothing. It only creates tremendous grief and guilt for the family members who are left.

A fourth bad response is to turn to a life of evil out of bitterness over a lack of justice (v. 21). This alienates one even further from God.

For Elihu, the only right response is to seek God with a humble heart, allowing him to teach us his ways (v. 22). He is a wise and omnipotent God with the right answers to all of life's problems. He deserves our attention and praise rather than criticism.

Possible Sermon Titles: "Oh, That God Would Test You to the Utmost!" "God Is Mighty but Despises No One"

IX. JOB 38–41: GOD'S SPEECHES

An Awesome God

We have finally reached the climax of the book of Job. God's two speeches in chapters 38–41 are the perfect response to the egotism of Elihu and the arrogance of Job and his three friends. Delivered from within a storm, the tone is awesome and overpowering. They leave Job and everyone who reads this book speechless. In addition, the content is completely unexpected. This provides one of the great surprise climaxes of all time.

There is a definite order to the speeches: (1) God's actions at the beginning of time in bringing the world into existence (38:4-11), (2) God's continuing governance of the world (38:12-38), (3) God's knowledge of and control over the animal kingdom (38:39–40:2), and (4) God's special fondness for the hippopotamus and the crocodile (40:15–41:34).

Between 40:2 and 40:15 God pauses briefly to allow Job to respond and then issues a short defense of his system of justice. The speeches are directed primarily at Job, although the other characters are listening in. The author also wants each reader to listen and respond.

There is certainly ample material here for a sermon titled "God as Creator" or "God as Sovereign" (→ previous chapter). The difference from Elihu's speech (chs. 32–37) is that now the Creator himself is doing the speaking rather than an outside observer with limited knowledge. And God knows far more about his creation than Elihu ever would.

IX. Job 38-41: God's Speeches

God's creation of the world was as effortless as if he were building a house. Each part was designed to fit in a specific place, from the foundation to the cornerstone. The divine blueprints were followed exactly.

Once the world was created, God established principles by which to operate it. For example, he orders the sun to rise each morning and the stars to be formed into recognizable constellations each evening. He sends the rain, hail, lightning, and snow at appropriate times.

The overall impression is that God is fully aware of what is going on in his world. He created it and continues to govern it. His wisdom about all of this is phenomenal, and his power to carry it out is overwhelming.

Preachers should be aware that God's speech is written in beautiful poetry. So make allowance for many figures of speech in describing God's acts of creation and governance.

God's knowledge and control of this world extend to the animal kingdom as well. Starting at 38:39, he lists a number of birds and animals he created that cannot be controlled or tamed by human beings. Animals such as the lion, the mountain goat, and the ostrich have unique characteristics that God provided just for them.

The final two animals God mentions are purposely placed last (40:15–41:34). The hippopotamus ("Behemoth" [40:15]) and the crocodile ("Leviathan" [41:1]) are two of the most fearsome and ugly animals in all of creation. Humanity certainly cannot tame them. Even hunting them may result in one's own death. Yet God likes them. He is proud of even these parts of his creation.

In both of God's speeches, he speaks with a tone of authority and challenge against anyone who would question his ability to do all of this. There are over seventy rhetorical questions that begin with hard-hitting interrogatives such as "Who is this . . . ?" (38:2), "Where were you . . . ?" (v. 4), "Who shut up . . . ?" (v. 8), and "Have you ever . . . ?" (v. 12). They figuratively pound out of Job any pretense that he knows what he is talking about when he questions God's actions. God is looking for an admission of ignorance by Job and an acknowledgment that he is very weak when compared to God's mighty power.

What can we take away from these intriguing poems?

1. God's Creation Is Stupendous

It is hard to find the right adjective to describe all of the beauty, the orderliness, and the complexity of God's masterful work of creation.

Humanity is making new scientific discoveries every year about the nature of our universe, from the smallest microscopic object to the vast extent of the universe. But we have only scratched the surface of what God knows about his creation. Nature still has many secrets. When one recognizes the power and wisdom required to put all of this in place, humility and gratefulness are the only proper responses.

2. God's Creation Is Well Ordered

Each animal has the characteristics needed to survive and to contribute something such as usefulness or beauty to the overall plan of the universe. God obviously thought all of this through ahead of time and planned everything down to the minutest detail.

3. God Likes Every Part of His Creation

Some animals are easier to like than others, but God likes them all just the way they are, even the ugliest and most fearsome. God also likes each of us just the way we are. He gave us the characteristics we have and expects us to glorify him by using our talents for his kingdom. The entire Bible speaks of God's care for every human being. We were created in his image (Gen. 1:27). We are offered salvation now from our sins (John 3:16). And we are invited to spend eternity with him in heaven (14:1-4; Rev. 22:12-17).

4. By Implication, God Holds Us Accountable for How We Treat What He Likes (See Also Gen. 1:28-30; Ps. 8)

This applies to the natural world as well as other human beings on this planet. If God likes each part of his creation, we should too. We should learn to appreciate all his handiwork, from the beautiful to the ugly, from the useful to the seemingly useless, and even the most annoying parts, such as gnats and mosquitoes. And we should work with God to preserve his creation for the generations that will follow us.

5. God Belongs at the Center of His Creation, Not Us

Throughout the dialogues, Job continually criticized God for not maintaining a proper order in the world, especially as it applied to justice (e.g., Job 24:1-12). Why had God not punished all the wicked and rewarded all the righteous? And why had God punished righteous Job? God did not seem to know how to govern properly.

IX. Job 38-41: God's Speeches

By arguing this way, Job was claiming to know more about these things than God did. In effect, he was attempting to demote God from his position as the creator and sovereign of the world and to elevate himself to a superior position of wisdom and authority. But God was not pleased with this attitude. His speech was purposely harsh in tone in order to challenge Job's self-centered claim. Job needed to learn that "the world simply does not revolve around Job and his special needs, but around God and the complex world that God has created and is in the business of sustaining" (Holbert 1999, 128).

In like manner, God expects all human beings to humbly acknowledge his awesomeness and rightful place at the center of creation. The universe is his, first and foremost. Job finally acknowledges this in his final speech (42:2-6).

Possible Sermon Titles: "Where Were You?" "Can You Do What God Can Do?" "Do You Have an Arm like God's?" "An Awesome God," "The Wild and Crazy Animal Kingdom," "God Sets the Record Straight," "God Likes You," "This Is My Father's World"

God's System of Justice (Job 40:6-14)

The questions Job raised in the dialogues about God's system of justice were appropriate. Every human being has asked them at least once. Why am I suffering? What did I do to deserve this? Why is life so unfair?

The only place in the book where God addresses these questions is in 40:6-14. And even here, God's explanation does not provide a completely satisfactory answer. But this is all we get, so this is an important section to address.

However, before we get to God's answer, we need to look again at the verses surrounding this passage. What is the purpose of God's description of his acts of creation, of his continuing governance of the world, and of his pleasure with the animal kingdom in chapters 38–41? To understand this, we need to be aware of how the ancient sages went about explaining difficult phenomena they had observed in the world.

The wisdom writers of Israel and other ancient cultures often used analogies to help people understand how life operated. They would set two totally different phenomena side by side. One was easily understood. The other was more difficult. The *known* helped to explain the meaning of the *unknown*. Here are some examples from the book of Proverbs.

- "Like clouds and wind without rain is one who boasts of gifts never given" (25:14).
- "As a dog returns to its vomit, so fools repeat their folly" (26:11).
- "As iron sharpens iron, so one person sharpens another" (27:17).
- "For as churning cream produces butter, and as twisting the nose produces blood, so stirring up anger produces strife" (30:33).

No doubt, the sages had great fun in putting together phenomena from totally different areas of life. The farther apart they were, the more interesting the proverb. Behind all of this, of course, was the belief that God created order in his universe. If we can discover the order in one area of life, we can then apply it to others (Rad 1972, 119-20). In the same manner, if we are ignorant in one area of life, we are probably ignorant in others.

That being the case, one of God's purposes in talking about various animals was to help Job recognize his ignorance about the animal kingdom. He then places alongside that ignorance Job's questions about injustice. "How can you discredit my system of justice," God asks, "if you cannot even understand the animal kingdom? If you are ignorant in one area of knowledge, Job, you are certainly ignorant in others as well. My wisdom and power in creating this universe are beyond your ability to comprehend. Likewise, my system of justice is something you will never understand."

God goes on, then, to challenge Job to create a better system of justice if he can. "If you think you know better than I do how to judge the world, give it a try. First, clothe yourself like a judge in royal garments and take your seat in the divine judgment room. Then as the people from across all of humanity pass by in front of you, identify every sinner. Pick out the wicked from the righteous. Look into their hearts, examine their motivations, and make a judgment about every person's spiritual condition. Finally, punish the wicked! Really punish them with a punishment they deserve! Send them all to Sheol! If you can do that correctly, then I will be the first to congratulate you. You will have earned the right to judge the world and the right to criticize my system of justice."

God knows Job cannot do this. And so does Job. He knows he is incapable of making good judgments about every human being. That is a task best left to God.

The point God is making is one each of us should take to heart. Even though we have each experienced what we regard as injustice, none of us are good judges of others. We cannot see into people's hearts. We are usually unaware of their motivations. And we would likely be swayed by intensely argued claims of righteousness. So none of us are qualified to criticize God's method of justice.

Jesus expanded this concept even further in the Sermon on the Mount (Matt. 7:1-5). He said that judging others opens the door for God to judge us in the same way. No one wants to be judged as we judge others. We would all rather be judged by someone like God, who has all the evidence and who is also merciful (Neh. 9:17).

The moral of the story is that God is the only one capable of judging people accurately (Deut. 32:35; Ps. 94:1-2; Rom. 12:19). Only he has the omniscience and omnipotence to carry it out. If questions arise with regard to our own unjust suffering, we will have to leave them with God. Whether he explains the cause of our suffering or not, only he knows best for each of our lives. Trust in him is what God is urging Job to do and what he recommends for each of us. That being so, it is absolutely astounding that almighty God offers to let measly Job create a system of justice to replace his own.

A further point this passage challenges us with is a caution about criticizing other people, especially those in leadership. We all have probably wished at some time to be king, president, prime minister, governor, mayor, or some other such leader for a day. We know exactly what we would do if we were in a leadership position to bring peace, justice, order, or compassion to some part of our world. We could certainly do a better job than whoever is in office right now. But those who criticize, even if it is constructive criticism, generally have no idea of the pressures and limitations faced by those in leadership. Unforeseen problems and the names of uncooperative personnel may never appear in the press to explain why things are not getting done. And leaders cannot speak of these limitations lest they look weak. As a result, leaders are often unwilling to seek advice from others.

God knows Job cannot create a better system of justice, but the very fact that he seeks Job's input is remarkable. It shows that God is always willing to listen patiently to our hurts and complaints. He must know that after we have gotten some things off our chests and allowed our emotions to settle, we will be much more willing to listen to him and acknowledge his rightful wisdom and power to govern the world.

IX. Job 38-41: God's Speeches

Possible Sermon Titles: "Would You Discredit My Justice?" "Why, God?" "If I Ruled the World," "God for a Day," "'Vengeance Is Mine,' Says the Lord," "Judge Not, That You Be Not Judged"

God's World

It is possible to use chapters 38–41 to preach on the relationship between religion and science. How should people reconcile their faith with their understanding of the natural world? This is a topic that has created a great deal of discussion within Christianity. There is no easy answer, and different people will approach the problem from different perspectives. But there are several basic questions the book addresses.

1. Why Does the World Exist?

The world exists because God wanted it to exist (38:4-11; Gen. 1:1). He was the one who thought it up and provided the blueprints for its design. And he went to work on it much like a builder going to work on a new building. It seemed very simple to him to lay a foundation and footings, align the dimensions with the blueprints, and set the cornerstone in place (Job 38:4-7). Any theory that disregards God's work as the Creator is false.

The exact method God used and the amount of time he took are topics science is still investigating. But the fact that he did it is a settled issue for all Christians.

2. Why Does the World Exist in This Form?

It exists in the form God chose at the beginning. All of its seas and skies, the star constellations, the seasons, day and night, and storms and lightning were designed by God. And then he filled his world with all kinds of strange-looking animal creations, each with unique characteristics. God made it all this way, and he delights in how it turned out. The world is beautiful in his eyes.

Not all people view the hippopotamus ("Behemoth") and the crocodile ("Leviathan") as beautiful, but God certainly does (40:15; 41:12). This is God's world through and through. Its design was chosen by him. And so to understand it, we must try to look at it through his eyes, not ours.

3. How Do We Gain the Wisdom to Understand This World?

There are two roads to truth about God's world. The first is revelation, and the second is science. In Job 28 the author makes it clear that if people want wisdom, they must ask God for it. No matter how skilled people may be in discovering information in some areas of life (such as mining), only God knows the way to real wisdom. Only he has the key that unlocks the door of understanding. And he has promised to reveal some of the mysteries of his creation if people will worship him and submit to his will. Genesis 1–3 is a good example of God's special revelation concerning creation.

The second road to truth is through science—that is, actually looking at the world and studying it and composing theories about how things operate. "Look at Behemoth," God says (Job 40:15). "You will see that this animal has tremendous strength and a huge belly and legs. Yet it feeds peacefully on grass and hides under the water during the day" (vv. 15-24, author's paraphrase). The implication is that we will find out many new things about the various parts of creation if we will just look at them. In doing so we will discover some of the great principles of order God has embedded in his universe, such as the principle of gravity. Thus there is a tremendous role for science to play in uncovering God's order. Humanity's curiosity and quest for knowledge will continue to spur us on to seek out truth wherever it may be found in God's world.

Both revelation and science are needed to complement each other in our search for truth. Those who focus on only one to the exclusion of the other soon find themselves out of balance. As the old saying goes, "All truth is God's truth." Whether the scientist or the theologian discovers it does not matter. All truth has its origin in God. Only the fact that God created an order to the natural world enables us to do science at all.

4. Why Do We Still Lack So Much Knowledge Concerning Our World?

The answer is because the nature of our world is far more complex than humans are capable of understanding. The repeated rhetorical questions in 38:39–39:30 emphasize the vast extent of human ignorance about so many parts of creation.

Additional truths about our world will continue to be discovered each year, but some may never be discovered. The fact that God spoke

IX. Job 38-41: God's Speeches

of wild animals such as the hippopotamus and the crocodile rather than cats and dogs indicates his desire to keep some knowledge to himself. God is free to govern his world in this way. This creates mystery, but it also creates excitement and assurance that we can fellowship with a God who has so much more knowledge than we do.

Possible Sermon Titles: "Why Does the World Exist?" "Behemoth and Leviathan: Two of God's Most Beautiful Animals!?" "Understanding God's World through Religion and Science," "Two Insightful and Complementary Ways of Looking at God's World"

X. JOB 40:3-5; 42:1-6: JOB'S RESPONSE TO GOD

Only a Novice Trying to Correct an Expert (Job 40:3-5; 42:1-6)

When God began to speak to Job (38:2-3), he told him right up front that this was going to be a vigorous debate. He told Job to prepare to defend himself like a strong man. The fact that God was speaking out of a storm cloud made the confrontation even more frightening. And then the more than seventy rhetorical questions God used to lambaste Job's knowledge only confirmed what Job had already feared about meeting with God (9:14-20, 32-35; 13:20-21; 23:15-16). God was simply too powerful for any human being to confront. No doubt, Job felt that God had flogged him both mentally and emotionally.

God also made it clear at the beginning of his speech that he was looking for a response (38:3). He wanted to know what Job was thinking. He was looking for some evidence that Job had changed his attitude toward God.

So after God's hard-hitting first speech (chs. 38–39) about (1) his awesome activities in creation, (2) his continued governance of the world, and (3) his knowledge of and delight in the animal kingdom, God paused to give Job an opportunity to respond (40:1-2).

What would you say in such a situation? What could anyone say in response to such an impressive speech?

Job did what most of us would do. He put his hand over his mouth and muttered something about his insignificance (vv. 3-5). He knew that

X. Job 40:3-5; 42:1-6: Job's Response to God

what he said would look very small compared to the grandeur of what God had just thundered from the heavens.

However, Job's feeble answer did not mask his disappointment over what God had left out of his speech. Deep inside, he was still struggling with the reasons for his suffering. To this point, God had said nothing about Job's losses. He had offered no sympathy, and he had given no word of hope or reassurance that his suffering would end. So even though Job was glad God had spoken to him, his heart still ached for some real comfort and hope for the future. We all would want the same.

From Job's perspective, God did not seem interested in reconciliation. He was only interested in battering Job into submission.

When Job fell silent, God began to speak again. He was not through confronting Job with his power. But first, as we looked at earlier, God spoke to Job's criticism of God's system of justice (40:7-14). God never explained how justice applied to Job, but he did emphasize that Job did not have the knowledge or the credentials to criticize God's method of administering justice. Job needed to acknowledge this before God was ready to offer reconciliation.

God's final words are two elegant poems on the hippopotamus ("Behemoth," vv. 15-24) and the crocodile ("Leviathan," 41:1-34). His purpose was to highlight the nature of the world he had created and to emphasize again Job's lack of knowledge about it. God knew everything, controlled everything, and liked everything in his creation.

Job's last speech is very short (42:1-6), but here God finally hears what he has been waiting to hear from Job's mouth. Job's confession centers around two main points: his new understanding of God and his new understanding of himself.

1. Job's New Understanding of God

Job had known God for all of his life, and in his earlier years he had been in communication with God on a regular basis. But the changes in his life brought about by the Examiner's calamities had produced in his heart hostility toward the Divine. And God's long silence had only exacerbated the situation. Now, however, Job's understanding of God had changed once again. He now *saw* God in new ways (42:5). God's magnificent speech in chapters 38–41 had forced him to a reevaluation.

First, God's power and wisdom are awesome. Job had always known that God was powerful and wise. But now that God had given him a

X. Job 40:3-5; 42:1-6: Job's Response to God

personal guided tour through the universe from its beginning days up until the present, Job's perspective had been broadened considerably. There was simply nothing God could not do (42:2). His ability to create, order, and govern the world was far beyond what Job ever imagined. Job admitted that his knowledge about such things was very limited.

Second, God knows what he is doing, even if we do not. He has "plans" (v. 3), and he can be trusted to do what is best for every person. Even times of suffering fit somewhere in God's plans. Job admits he was wrong to criticize God about his system of justice. Justice was something only God understood and was able to carry out.

Third, Job already knew that God causes suffering in the lives of the wicked as a judgment on their sin. But he had never considered that God allows/causes suffering in the lives of the righteous for reasons other than sin. Job did not know what these reasons were as they applied to him. They were hidden in God's mysterious nature. Newsom notes that people today still have great difficulty in accepting this reality in their own lives. The following lengthy quote states a truth about life that many are afraid to admit.

> Like the characters in the book of Job, many people are reluctant to confront the reality that human beings cannot secure their lives and their families against harm. We do not want to see that bad things happen to good people. Yet horrible things can happen. . . . We all know that to be true, and yet we resist it. . . . Drunk drivers exist, but why must one kill *my* child? Cancer is a reality, but why must it strike *my* spouse? The seeming randomness of such events is terrifying, and so we cling to interpretive paradigms of experience that will mask the reality. . . . Job's friends employed a number of such frameworks, which allowed disaster to be seen as moral discipline, punishment, etc. Job rejected those frameworks but embraced an alternative, legal paradigm that allowed him to declare the disaster morally wrong and to have someone to blame. All of these paradigms allowed them not to see what they were afraid to see—that the chaotic is an irreducible aspect of creation that must be taken into account in any adequate understanding of experience. To that extent, their moral paradigms served them as a means of denial. (1996, 630)

Fourth, God is someone who desires fellowship with his followers. He does attempt to communicate with each of us. The fact that God appeared to Job at the Uz city dump and delivered a message to him personally confirmed in Job's mind that God really did want to renew fellowship with him. As with Job, we may not hear what we want to hear or what we expect to hear, but God will tell us what *he* wants us to hear. And that along with his presence will be sufficient until such time that God decides to reveal more.

2. Job's New Understanding of Himself

God's long tour through the universe had also enlightened Job on new ways of looking at his own place in the cosmos.

First, he now readily admitted that his knowledge about God was very limited (42:3). Previously, he had thought that he knew as much as God about how to run the world. God's treatment of Job was a prime example of God's inability to judge properly. But in 40:7-14 God had challenged Job to act like God if he thought he could—to do the things God does, only do them better. Job knew that was an impossibility for him. Now he knew that God's knowledge was far greater than his, and it would always remain so. He felt humiliated by his earlier criticisms in the dialogues of God's lack of knowledge.

Second, he acknowledged he had spoken too hastily. Instead of waiting for God to speak and then listening to what he had to say, Job had filled the air with words "without knowledge" (42:3). He knew he was just as guilty as his three friends of jumping to hasty conclusions without evidence.

Third, he recognized that his attitude toward God needed changing. He had been too arrogant and overly confident of his rightness in the dialogues. His approach to God had even been hostile at times. Now he had returned to his earlier attitude of trust in God. The one who had created him and this magnificent world was worthy of his respect and worship.

Fourth, while not explicitly stated in verses 2-6, there is an implied recognition from Job that God now accepted him as one of his beloved creatures and desired reconciliation and fellowship. No doubt, Job was as surprised as we are by the content of God's speeches. Except for God's brief challenge to Job concerning justice (40:7-14), the entire speech deals with parts of the natural world. Undoubtedly, Job's ears were all primed to hear God say something about his supposed sin or to question his claims of innocence (ch. 31). But God said not a word about Job's personal morality. Job had to have interpreted God's silence as confirmation that his claims of moral innocence were correct. And if God was willing to pronounce him morally clean, he was more than ready to admit his ignorance of God's plans and apologize for his belligerent behavior.

All four of these reasons contributed to Job's sense of humiliation after listening to God in the storm. He felt like a novice trying to correct an expert. Now Job knew for certain that God had been right all along and that he had been wrong. Confession and apology were what God was looking for, and Job freely gave God both in his final speech. As God saw it, Job was now ready for reconciliation. This will occur in the epilogue.

Like Job, we all need times to reevaluate our understanding of God and of ourselves. We can easily develop a lackadaisical attitude toward God and an overconfidence in our own ability to direct our lives. While we may think that God was overly harsh on Job in chapters 38–41, God knew exactly what he was doing. His grand tour through the universe interspersed with numerous rhetorical questions forced Job to admit his limited knowledge about justice and about God's greater power and wisdom in running the world. Sometimes the crises in our lives can force us to make the same admission.

Possible Sermon Titles: "Now My Eye Sees You," "Only a Novice," "My Understanding of God Is Too Small," "Troubles Have Always Been a Part of Life"

Who Am I? (Job 42:1-6)

In 42:1-6, Job is wrestling with one of the greatest questions of all time: "Who are we as human beings?" And more specifically: "Who am I?" (McKenna 1986, 309). What is the purpose of my life? Where do I fit in the universe? My physical strength is very weak. My knowledge of the natural world is very limited. And my time on earth is very short. The odds seem stacked against me. So what am I worth? Seemingly nothing.

The question about the meaning of our existence is one that all human beings ask of themselves during their formative years. As young people grow up and try to establish their own identities apart from their parents, they often struggle with finding a good answer to this question.

Job was certainly well beyond his formative years, but his experiences with suffering and loss had shaken the foundations of his faith. He was forced to ask this question again.

The answer he comes to is one we all should consider for our own lives. It includes the following points.

1. I Certainly Am Not Omnipotent like God (Job 42:2)

God can do whatever he wants. Nothing holds him back. No one is stronger than he is, and no obstacle is too big to get in his way. God's tour through creation and the natural world had convinced Job that God had more than enough power to run his universe.

2. I Certainly Am Not Omniscient like God (Job 42:3a)

God's knowledge of the animal kingdom had confirmed to Job that he knew very little about the world in which he lived. There were many strange animals about which he knew next to nothing. God seemed to know even the smallest detail about every animal and bird. Job admitted that God knew far more about nature than he did. Job also recognized for the first time that God's knowledge of the natural world sprang from his care for all of creation. God really did like the world he had brought into being.

3. I Certainly Am Not All Wise like God (Job 42:3b)

Job now recognized that he should have kept his mouth closed. He should have listened to God instead of trying to tell him how to run his universe. This included the world of morality. God was concerned about justice, and he was a just God. Job needed to quit criticizing God for causing his own suffering and for what he saw as injustice in the world around him. Instead, he should trust God to do what is right and just in all situations in life.

Anyone listening to God's speeches (chs. 38–41) or reading them now would probably come to the same conclusion as Job. God is so far above human capabilities that humans seem almost worthless. Job's reaction in 42:6b was normal. He despised himself for the things he had said against God and his plans. They were spoken out of ignorance and weakness. He regretted having said them, for God's speeches had shown him a better human response to God. He had changed his mind from criticism to reverence and respect for God.

X. Job 40:3-5; 42:1-6: Job's Response to God

4. So Who Am I, Then? I Am Just a Small Creature, but One That God Likes

The book of Job does not spell out all the ways God wants to relate to his creatures, but it does imply that God cares deeply about all parts of creation (chs. 38–41). Even though our strength, our knowledge, and our time are limited, God has need of them. He created us like this because he likes us like this.

Psalm 8 carries this thought even further. In spite of the tremendous difference between God's magnificence and human insignificance, God still regards us as having worth. We are *nothing* when compared to God and his universe. But God, in an act of astounding grace, chose to regard us as *something*, creating us just a little lower than God himself and crowning us with his glory and honor and giving us dominion over all the works of his hands.

In other words, humans are very special to God. There is no need to hang our heads with a sense of worthlessness. God knows we are frail, but we are also of great value to him. We can take confidence in that and live our lives with the assurance that our lives matter to him.

Job finally got it. God had finally gotten through to him so that he saw God in a new light. His personal encounter with God would mean changes in his attitude toward and perspective about God, but he was more than willing to make these changes if it provided reconciliation between them.

Now Job could go on living—not because he knew the cause of his suffering and could do something about it—but because he had had a personal encounter with almighty God (see also "How Can Faith Be Maintained When Life Goes Topsy-Turvy?" in Bowes 2018, 409-11). This is the same reason the Israelites believed in God. Throughout their history, they had experienced God's compassion and love over and over again (Ps. 86:15). Their continual encounters with him had convinced them that he cared about them and desired their fellowship.

For the same reason, people believe in God today. His compassion and love for all humanity were proven on the cross. And his desire to fellowship with us right now leads him to encounter every human being on multiple occasions (Ezek. 18:23; 33:17; John 3:16-17; Rom. 2:4; 1 Cor. 1:9; 1 Tim. 2:4; 2 Pet. 3:9). A personal encounter with this almighty God who cares about us is the starting point and the necessary founda-

X. Job 40:3-5; 42:1-6: Job's Response to God

tion for any relationship with him. And continued encounters are needed to maintain our fellowship with him and our faith through the storms and sufferings of life.

Possible Sermon Titles: "Who Am I?" "One of Life's Greatest Questions," "A Personal Encounter with Almighty God"

XI. JOB 42:7-17: EPILOGUE

And He Lived Happily Ever After (Job 42:7-17)

There is no question that Job's life ends on the same idyllic plain as in the prologue, only now he is even more blessed than before. His extended family and community returned to fellowship with him and pay their respects. Over a period of many years, his earlier wealth doubled in size, and another ten children in the same proportion of seven sons and three daughters were born into his family. And God gave him double the ideal length of life for a righteous person in the OT (Ps. 90:10).

What are we to make of this? Certainly we are pleased for Job. Probably every reader of the book is glad to see that Job's suffering finally comes to an end. We all know he deserved a better life than what he suffered after the disasters in the prologue. In spite of intense pain and anguish, he had proven his integrity on countless occasions. He had refused to be swayed by the mistaken advice of his wife, his three friends, and Elihu. Their words contained much truth, but they missed the whole point of Job's suffering because they were unaware of the divine conversation in the prologue.

However, what about us? Are we to assume that God will bless us in the same measure as he blessed Job if we stay true to him through our times of suffering? The answer is no! Job's blessings were unique to him. For some saints, there are years of sickness and an early death. For others, there is continual poverty. For still others, there is never any recognition of worth, much less greatness. God does not provide each person with the same kinds of rewards as Job. The whole point of the prologue was to show that rewards and punishments are not needed to bribe people into faithful service to God.

So what can we learn from these final verses in the book of Job?

XI. Job 42:7-17: Epilogue

1. God Desires to Be in Relationship with Every Human Being (Job 42:7-9)

God wanted to fellowship with Job—his favorite supersaint. The only reason he remained silent in response to Job's requests for a meeting was to test the level of Job's faith. Job had said some pretty nasty things to God that seemed to indicate he had lost his trust in God. God was looking for some evidence that Job was sorry for these outbursts and had changed his attitude toward God. When he finally heard Job's words in 42:1-6, he knew Job had ceased his complaints and criticisms and was ready for reconciliation. He immediately resumed calling Job "my servant" (vv. 7-8) as he had done in the prologue (1:8; 2:3).

God also desired to be in relationship with the three friends. They had not spoken the truth about God, even though they thought they were right. They needed to admit their "folly" (42:8) and return to fellowship with God, for they had become estranged from him.

God graciously offered the friends a way back to reconciliation. He required them to do two things. First, they had to offer a huge sacrifice of seven bulls and seven rams. By doing so, they were admitting that their speeches had been very offensive to God. They had misdiagnosed Job's problems, they had not shown compassion, and they had not delivered the message God wanted Job to hear, even though they claimed to speak for God.

Second, they had to ask Job to intercede for them with God. This required a confession on their part of their offenses against both Job and God. Job would then present their confessions to God, acting as their intermediary and praying for their spiritual restoration. They needed to be reconciled with Job before God would consider their reconciliation with him.

God provides a pathway to reconciliation for every human being. No one has been denied access to God. We must find that pathway and follow it if we want to maintain fellowship with him.

2. A Life of Integrity Is Not Dependent on One's Circumstances

Reputations are fickle. They come and go quickly, many times for unknown reasons or reasons beyond our control. The same can be said about one's success, well-being, or recognition. We usually have no control over what life brings us or what people say about us or do to us. Sickness, poverty, accidents, cruel mistreatment, slander, and the like may happen to anyone, but they need not and should not affect our integrity.

Job's reputation was outstanding in the early part of his life. It sank to awful depths after the calamities in the prologue. But then it rose again to even higher heights in the epilogue. All the while, Job continued to maintain his integrity. This was a personal choice he made, an inner commitment to a quality of life. Such is God's desire for each of us.

3. A Meaningful Epitaph Is a Great Conclusion to One's Life (Job 42:10-17)

Verses 12-16 are typical of information found in most obituaries today. By the end of his life Job had gained enormous wealth. He had fathered another family of ten children, three of whom had become beautiful women. He was survived by numerous grandchildren and great grandchildren. And he had lived to 140, twice the ideal age. All of this was the result of God's blessings on his life. He was once again a super-saint, the greatest of his generation. No doubt, he was gratified at his well-lived life, especially so after his earlier suffering and loss.

Verse 17 is different. It is more similar to an epitaph—a very short summary of his life that could fit on a tombstone. Job's epitaph reads as follows: "an old man and full of years" (v. 17). Job was certainly an old man when he died, well beyond the normal life span of a person in the OT period. But he also had filled his life with good things. The phrase "full of years" is literally "satiated of days" (AT). It is also found in the epitaphs for Abraham (Gen. 25:8), Isaac (Gen. 35:29), David (1 Chron. 29:28), and Jehoiada the priest (2 Chron. 24:15). These people were all viewed as great heroes of the OT. The phrase means that one's years of life on this earth were packed full of good and righteous activities. It implies that one's life was pleasing to God.

We all amass various amounts of possessions and honors in life, and hopefully we enjoy the occupations we have chosen and the family relationships of which we are a part. These pieces of information will be placed in our obituary. But what will our epitaph read? What short bits of information will summarize the life we have lived while here on this earth? Most people have only their dates of birth and death on their tombstones, with a dash in between. The dash stands for all the activities that have occurred between birth and death. What activities does your dash represent?

XI. Job 42:7-17: Epilogue

Job's dash included his many days of suffering and agony as well as his years of wealth and honor. But even more, it represented his faithful service to God. The author described him in the prologue as "blameless and upright"; a man who "feared God and shunned evil" (Job 1:1). In other words, his days had been satiated with righteous and holy living. He well deserved the honor that came with this phrase belonging to the OT's saints.

Possible Sermon Titles: "Reconciliation with God," "Epitaph for a Supersaint: An Old Man and Full of Years," "What Do You Want Printed on Your Tombstone?"

CONCLUSION

A sermon on Job's epitaph (42:17) could be the final sermon in the series. But if the preacher feels a need for more of a summarizing sermon, there are several options available. One is to highlight the major theological themes in the book, either in one sermon or several. Here are some possibilities.

Major Theological Themes

1. The Nature of God

Focusing on God provides a natural conclusion to the book. His awesome power, unfathomable wisdom, and incredible orderliness are on display throughout the book. One can draw especially from God's speeches (chs. 38–41) and Elihu's speech (chs. 32–37). The following four points from my commentary provide a ready outline (Bowes 2018, 407).

- God is the Creator and Sustainer of the universe. His wisdom and power to accomplish this are beyond human comprehension, for he operates on a far superior level than humankind.
- God embedded his order in both the physical world and the world of morality. To humanity, the world may sometimes look chaotic, haphazard, or unjust, but God knows what he is doing. He has a plan.
- God is a just Judge in his overall governance of the world. However, for reasons known only to him, he does sometimes allow the suffering of the innocent and the prosperity of the wicked (*injustice*, as humanity sees it) to happen. Whether God also sees it as injustice is unknown.

- God has the freedom to act as he wishes. He can bless or he can punish or he can choose to remain inactive. No one can put God in a box or tell him what to do. This creates mysteries and paradoxes about some aspects of the universe, especially in the moral realm.

Job lived a long, successful life after his restoration described in the epilogue. But he eventually died. And the other human characters in the book of Job all died and disappeared. But God remains forever. The curtain never closes on his daily activities. He has committed himself to maintaining his/our world until the end of time. His steadiness and faithfulness on this matter are a quality upon which human beings can depend. He is "the same yesterday and today and forever" (Heb. 13:8). God is the real hero of the book.

Possible Sermon Titles: "The Same, Yesterday and Today and Forever," "The Real Hero of the Book of Job"

2. The Nature of the Cosmos

The nature of our world is a topic worthy of a preacher's comments. In the Western world people seem to divide themselves into two camps concerning a proper human understanding of nature. Some see the natural world as something to be used and exploited for human benefit. They have no problem with paving over wetlands to provide a new subdivision or shopping center. And climate change is a topic that infuriates them because it interrupts their right to make money and consume resources for personal pleasure.

On the other extreme are those who treat nature as something to be worshipped. Stepping on an ant and killing a spider are activities to be avoided. Climate change is a topic of the utmost significance because it could mean the end of life on this planet.

In contrast, the book of Job provides a healthy and balanced look at our world through the eyes of God. He created it and ordered it according to principles that science has only begun to understand. And he likes his world with all of its crazy-looking creatures. But most of all he likes the part of his creation called humanity. And he wants to be in fellowship with every human being every day. Job's suffering was a major concern to God, even though Job never felt like it.

God holds humanity accountable for taking care of his world. This world was not created to be exploited and destroyed by human beings. It was created for God's enjoyment and the well-being of all his creatures. And he expects his creatures to work alongside him in ensuring its preservation and fruitfulness (Gen. 2:15) (for additional comments on this topic, see "The Nature of the Cosmos" in Bowes 2018, 408).

Possible Sermon Titles: "God's World," "The Nature of the World in Which We Live," "Exploitation or Worship? What Is a Biblical Understanding of Our Responsibility to Planet Earth?"

3. The Nature of Suffering

Unjust suffering is the topic most people associate with Job, and it is a relevant topic in any generation. Why not conclude with a sermon on this topic?

Bad stuff happens. And it often occurs at the worst possible moment. We are told to prepare ourselves for it, but no one is really prepared for the difficult times in life. We expect to enjoy successful lives if we are obedient to God and endeavoring to contribute to his kingdom. But unpleasant things do happen in life. And sometimes they seem very unjust and unfair. All the human characters in the book of Job struggled with trying to understand how this could happen.

The friends could not believe that a righteous person could experience suffering, especially such horrible suffering as Job had endured. That would be unjust of God. Since God was a just God, their logical reasoning led them to blame Job, accusing him of some great sin that had caused God to punish him. What other explanation could there be? But they failed miserably in their analysis, as many people still do today. (1) They misunderstood God's nature. (2) They refused to believe Job's testimony. They thought he was lying about his moral innocence. (3) They failed to allow for exceptions to the general rules of life (see "The Wisdom Theology Is Inadequate to Explain All of Life's Troubles" in Bowes 2018, 411). (4) They were lacking all the evidence about Job's case, specifically the conversation in the prologue between God and the Examiner.

Even Job failed to understand accurately his situation. He, too, thought his suffering was due to some divine punishment. The difference between him and his friends was that he knew he was righteous. So why would God want to punish him?

Conclusion

The connection between suffering and punishment is one that people still struggle with today. This connection must be broken in our minds before real understanding can take place. God does sometimes punish for sin. There are plenty of examples in Scripture. But to attribute every type of suffering to divine punishment does a disservice to God. It shows a lack of understanding of his character.

It is true that God is ultimately responsible for everything in life because he is the Creator. He set the world in motion at the beginning, and it continues to operate according to his principles. Earthquakes, floods, hurricanes, and volcanoes, as well as bacteria and viruses, have always been a part of his plan, at least since the first sin in the garden of Eden. These are part of the stuff that our world experiences continually. And then, of course, there is death itself, which we know will affect every living thing sooner or later.

Therefore, if bad stuff is inevitable, what should be our reaction to it?

The first human reaction to suffering is usually to seek out the cause. It is often thought that if we can name the cause and explain the reasons for our troubles, we will then know who to blame and be able to direct our grief/anger away from ourselves. This mental exercise always begins with the word *why*. Our attempts to go down this pathway may or may not be successful, for there are a multitude of reasons why people experience pain and suffering, such as natural disasters, other people's bad choices or carelessness, and divine discipline (for additional reasons, see "The Nature of Suffering" in Bowes 2018, 408-9).

God often leaves us without an explanation, as he did with Job. But even if we put our finger on a definite cause, that does not mitigate the distress that suffering causes. There will be times of weeping in everyone's life. And there will be feelings of anxiety, frustration, failure, complete exhaustion, and even anger, as well as times of intense physical pain. That being so, our emphasis in life should not be on doing everything possible to prevent cancer, financial reverses, burglaries, slander, death, and so forth. That pathway ends in fear, depression, and failure.

A second reaction to suffering is to surround oneself with "the traditional rituals and formulas" that one's culture practices (Newsom 1996, 383). In the case of grief that comes with death, Israelite culture followed certain rituals such as wailing, putting on sackcloth, and sprinkling dust on one's head. In American Protestantism there are also certain rituals associated with death, including a viewing of the body of the deceased, an appropriate religious service, a trip to the cemetery where final goodbyes and tears are expressed, and a meal with family and friends where life is supposed to return to normal. Such rituals are expected and can be comforting, but not always. It is ever so hard to fill the emptiness death leaves behind.

A third reaction to suffering that begins to integrate the sufferer back into society is to surround that person with close friends or a support group dedicated to helping sufferers. One should not count on friends like Job's friends to be of much help. They are only interested in solving the *why* question. One should look for friends who know how to listen and empathize in order to aid the process of emotional healing.

A fourth reaction is one that some people have found very helpful. Newsom describes it as "integrating the disrupting and disorienting experiences of suffering into a larger understanding of life and world" by refusing to allow suffering to have the last word (1996, 382-83). Some have found immense satisfaction in looking for ways that hurtful experiences can develop into something good. For example, some have started foundations or supported causes such as cancer research with the thought that someone's death should not be in vain. In this way the dead still live on through the actions of the living.

Finally, in order to move on beyond the crises of life, one must find new "grounds for hope beyond suffering" (Newsom 1996, 383). Suffering does not have "meaning and purpose" in and of itself (572). One cannot honestly say, "God meant this awful tragedy to happen to me to teach me a lesson." We simply do not know the causes of many of our troubles or whether they have any purpose at all. Some just happen.

However, each of us can find meaning and purpose by looking beyond our present troubles to something outside of them, specifically to the hope God offers both in this life and in the next (Rom. 8:26-28). This hope is based on God's power over suffering and all of its causes and his significant presence during suffering that can fill one's emptiness (Newsom 1996, 573). It may take some time for the pain to diminish, for suffering does not automatically go away by itself after a certain length of time. The grief from death and tragedy may linger for years. But eventually the clouds will part and the sun will begin to shine again, even if only for a brief moment on the first day.

Attitudes play an extremely important role in helping people deal with suffering. A person who focuses on self and pity and the injustices of life seldom moves past whining and complaint. But attitudes that seek to engage with God and the world in creative ways usually help people to put their troubles behind them after a period of time and move on to new challenges in life.

People have found hope in any number of places, such as (1) a new friend or a longtime friend, (2) a new hobby or an old hobby that has been neglected, (3) a new place to live or a remodeling of the old place, (4) a new cause to support or an old cause that needs new energy, (5) a new experience with God or a fresh return to an old relationship with one's heavenly Father, and (6) a new awareness of the joys of life after death or a greater appreciation for a life that has ceased but that still lives on in one's heart and in the afterlife. God will help us find a new and refreshing source of hope if we will allow him the time and the opportunity to do so.

Sometimes hope surprises us suddenly out of the blue. In the same week that my wife's father passed away, our youngest daughter announced she was pregnant with our first grandchild. The ending of one life and the beginning of another were not something we could have predicted or planned, but God providentially brought the two events together.

Other times hope already lies within us. It just needs a catalyst to bring it to our attention. A life of personal integrity is like a field that has been well maintained over many years of time. Hope is like a seed that lies dormant in the soil of our lives until God causes it to spring forth in the moment of need. Building a life of personal integrity that can withstand the storms of life is not something that happens overnight. It starts with a personal choice and then develops over years of life's experiences. It is based on trust in God's promises to be with us (Josh. 1:5, 9) and to provide the strength we are lacking in times of trouble (Isa. 40:28-31).

Possible Sermon Titles: "Bad Stuff Happens," "Suffering Is Not the End of All Things Good"

The Purpose of the Book of Job

Another option for a concluding sermon is to comment on the main purpose of the book and how it should impact readers today. There are two questions the book tries to address: "Why do people serve God?" and "How can faith be maintained when life goes topsy-turvy?" (see

Conclusion

Bowes 2018, 409-11). Both questions have clear answers in the book that should benefit any contemporary congregation.

1. Why Do People Serve God?

There are many reasons why people serve God, including (1) the desire to go to heaven rather than to hell, (2) the recognition that our own efforts to create a meaningful life for ourselves have failed, (3) a deep conviction and sorrow for the sinful things we have done and said against God and other human beings, and (4) the desire to be in fellowship with the One who created us. Some of the reasons people give are completely off base. One that has infected the Christian faith in recent years is the belief that God always rewards his followers with blessings. Therefore, one will live a better life if one serves God. And one will avoid all kinds of diseases and troubles by serving God. In other words, religion survives because it benefits the self-interest of the believer.

This is the crux of the issue that the Examiner raised with God in the prologue. However, it not only belittles the quality of human faith but also attacks God's character by portraying him as a *rich uncle* who passes out favors to his followers in order to secure their services. God's willingness to let the Examiner test Job, even though he knew it would cause Job intense suffering, arose from a desire to prove to heaven and earth that people can and should serve God for reasons other than self-interest. Job was his prime example that faithful obedience to God in response to his love produced a divine-human fellowship that was far more attractive and beneficial to human beings than any reward God could bestow.

2. How Can Faith Be Maintained When Life Goes Topsy-Turvy?

This is the practical question Job wrestled with in the chapters following the prologue. He was forced to endure speech after speech from friends who were trying to help him but who misdiagnosed the cause of his suffering and became entrapped in their own agendas. They were of no help to him at all.

The only way Job received help was through a personal encounter with God. It was then that he saw he could trust his life with God. As God took Job on a tour of the universe and the animal kingdom, Job began to realize that God really did know what he was doing and that this God really did care about him. Once that was settled, it was only a short distance to admitting he had criticized God wrongly. He willingly apologized for what he had said and resubmitted his life to God. He continued to live a righteous life in fellowship with God for his remaining years on earth.

Your emphasis here should be on the importance of a personal relationship with God that undergirds a person's soul in times of trouble and anguish. But there are other helps in other parts of Scripture that one can draw upon when going through the fiery furnace. "God's continual presence and love (Josh 1:9; John 14:16-21), the support of the body of Christ (John 15:12, 17; Gal 6:2), and the encouragement that there is a limit to what God will allow (1 Cor 10:13)" are some of the other means of support and assistance to be found in the Bible (see Bowes 2018, 412).

3. God Gives and God Takes Away

The author then uses his answers to the two questions above to critique the wisdom theology found in other parts of the OT, particularly with regard to the topic of retributive justice. This topic is still widely misunderstood today in Christian circles. It needs to be addressed from time to time in any preacher's sermon schedule (see "The Validity of Retributive Justice" in Bowes 2018, 412-13).

God does bless and/or punish people on occasion. As Job said, "God gives and God takes away" (1:21, author's paraphrase). The reasons he does so are not always evident. And it is fruitless to speculate about this mysterious side of his nature. He does what he does for reasons known only to him. This sometimes creates situations that seem unjust to human observers. Why would God allow one of his saints to contract cancer and die at an early age? Job's friends were caught in the wisdom theology's belief that people always reap what they sow. Although the rule is generally true, as Job learned, God does not always treat people in this way. If anything, God leans toward the side of mercy in his interactions with human beings. He sends the sun and the rain on both the righteous and the unrighteous (Matt. 5:45). None can legitimately accuse God of treating them worse than they deserve, but all can praise God for treating them better than they deserve.

Possible Sermon Topics: "Why Read Job?" "Lessons from the Life of a Supersaint"

Trust in God

A third option for a concluding sermon is to expand on what the book of Job teaches us about trust in God. When one reads through the book for the first time, the natural reaction is that this is the goofiest divine being that ever existed. First, God (through his agent the Examiner) causes his best saint to endure horrendous tragedy—the loss of his possessions, the loss of his children, the loss of his reputation, and then the loss of his health. In very short order God reduces Job's status to that of a wretched pauper whom no one wants to be around.

And then, when God finally decides to enter the story and resolve the crisis in Job's life, he never says one word of comfort. He could have said he had ten thousand angels ready to minister to Job's needs. He could have said that the people of God were praying for him. He could have just put his arm around Job and lovingly held him close. That's what we would like God to do for us.

Instead, using a series of approximately seventy rhetorical questions, God takes Job on a grand tour of the universe, beginning with creation. He literally thunders from the heavens that he brought the entire universe into existence. He notes that he now controls the stars and the weather. And then God tours the animal kingdom, describing the intimate details of a host of wild animals he created and likes. "What's the purpose of this?" we ask. "Why do we need to know about the hippopotamus and the crocodile?" It is to show Job that God can be trusted in every aspect of life. He planned the universe and ordered it down to the smallest detail. In modern terminology, from the largest galaxy to the smallest particle in the atom, God put everything in place. And he continues to maintain it each day, summoning the sun to rise each morning and sending the clouds and the rain when needed to water the farmers' crops.

By implication, God was saying to Job (and to us), "I know you are going to have suffering in life, including the death of family members [remember, Job lost ten children]. But trust me to watch over your life. Just as I take care of my universe each day, I will take care of you. I will go before you and behind you and around you and with you, even through the 'valley of the shadow of death' [Ps. 23:4, KJV]." Trust in God is the only pathway that gets us through the trials and tribulations of life.

Conclusion

The reason Job was so angry at his situation and at God was because he had not been able to rule horrible suffering out of his life. He had assumed, as did the three friends, that all the troubles of life can be avoided if one is blameless before God and turns away from evil (Job 1:1). He was further angered by God's silence in response to his questions and pleas. But Job learned through the school of hard knocks that "God does not offer insurance against all harm" (Newsom 1996, 535). Every human being, whether a follower of God or not, has experienced or will experience some sort of tragedy. That's the negative but realistic side of life.

However, there is a positive side expressed in 28:28 (also in Ps. 111:10; Prov. 1:7; 9:10; 15:33). By practicing what the author calls "the fear of the Lord," God offers to each of us a small measure of his wisdom that enables us to see some of the big picture of life from his perspective and to experience inner peace through his overwhelming love, presence, strength, and encouragement.

I have tried to refrain from personal examples throughout the book, but perhaps one would be appropriate as a conclusion. A number of years ago, my wife and I were praying about a difficult situation we were facing. I agonized with God over this for a year and a half, thinking at times I had prayed through about it and then going back to the agony again. One night I woke up at 2:00 a.m. I tossed this situation around in my mind for two hours and then finally got up at 4:00 a.m. so that Ginger could get some sleep. I made my way to my study and began to look for a Scripture to give me some comfort. That's what Christians often do in times of trouble.

I began in Genesis with the creation story. I thanked God for giving me life. Then I moved to Joshua 1:5, one of my favorite passages: "As I was with Moses, so I will be with you; I will never leave you nor forsake you." I said, "That's great Lord, that you're with me, but I want you to answer my prayer."

I turned to the Psalms thinking that there's got to be a psalm for me today. I read Psalm 23 and maybe a dozen more, but nothing seemed to fit my situation.

So I turned to Isaiah and read those great words from 40:28-31:
Do you not know?
    Have you not heard?
The LORD is the everlasting God,
    the Creator of the ends of the earth.

> He will not grow tired or weary,
>> and his understanding no one can fathom.
> He gives strength to the weary
>> and increases the power of the weak.
> Even youths grow tired and weary,
>> and young men stumble and fall;
> but those who hope in the Lord
>> will renew their strength.
> They will soar on wings like eagles;
>> they will run and not grow weary,
>> they will walk and not be faint.

I said, "Thank you, God, for promising to renew my strength when I am weary, but what are you going to do about my problem?"

I moved on to Jeremiah and read about his discouragement over his persecution. I thought, "That's me. I'm just as discouraged as Jeremiah."

I finally got to the NT and began to skim through Jesus's ministry—one miracle after another, one good deed after another. Jesus always seemed to have the right answer for the people who approached him about their problems. Why couldn't he provide one for me?

I read through some of the miracles in the book of Acts. And then I started reading Paul's letters. I remembered that the book of Philippians was one of his most positive books, and toward the end there are some great words of promise and hope. I read through the entire book that night. In chapter 4 I slowed down because a number of great words of promise began to appear. "Rejoice in the Lord always. I will say it again: Rejoice!" (v. 4). I responded, "That's nice, God, but I don't feel like rejoicing tonight." "Do not be anxious about anything, but in every situation, by prayer and petition, with thanksgiving, present your requests to God. And the peace of God, which transcends all understanding, will guard your hearts and your minds in Christ Jesus" (vv. 6-7). "But I can't quit worrying, Lord. I have presented my need to you multiple times, and I don't have an answer."

And then I read verse 9: "Keep on doing the things that you have learned and received and heard and seen in me, and the God of peace will be with you" (NRSV). I stopped and read it again. And God said to me, "That's my verse to you for today, and that's all I'm going to give you about your problem." What God seemed to be saying to me was this: "You know exactly how to live the Christian life. Keep on doing that today and the next day and the next day, and trust me to work out your problems. If you do your part, I will do mine."

I never did get a divine answer to my problem, and it never worked out as I had hoped. But I learned the importance of striving daily to do his will as best as I understood it. And I learned how to turn my hands over and let go of my anxieties and just trust in him a day at a time.

Job finally learned that lesson as well. God never answered his request for a reason for his suffering. But he was satisfied that he could go on living after his personal encounter with God. His trust in the Lord had been renewed. Now Job "can do something much more important than explain his sorrows. He can live with them" (McKeating 1971, 246). And so can we.

Possible Sermon Titles: "Trust in God," "God's Message to Us through Job," "Living with Our Questions and Sorrows," "Put Your Hand in the Hand of the Man Who Stilled the Water"[*]

---

[*]Gene MacLellan, "Put Your Hand in the Hand," © 1970 (Renewed 1998) Beechwood Music of Canada. All rights for the U.S.A. controlled and administered by Beechwood Music Corp. All rights reserved. International copyright secured.

APPENDIX: BIBLICAL ILLITERACY

The first sentence in the introduction is not intended as a put-down of contemporary pastors. Most of them spend hours each week diligently seeking God's guidance and poring through commentaries for next Sunday's sermon. I know all about this difficult task, for I served as a pastor myself for over ten years.

Rather, the first sentence is meant to sound the alarm that a scarcity of good preaching from the OT has major consequences for American Christianity, one of which is a rising tide of biblical illiteracy. Fewer and fewer Christians know even the basic facts about the major characters and events in the Bible. And if they do not know the basic facts and have a clear understanding of the theological positions derived from those facts, how can they effectively influence their society with the message of the gospel?

In 1997 an article of mine dealing with this topic appeared in *The Preacher's Magazine* (Bowes 1997). The article was based on a survey of 262 freshmen students who enrolled in BL101 Biblical Literature and History at Northwest Nazarene College (now Northwest Nazarene University) in the 1994-95 school year. There were thirty questions on the survey, thirteen from the OT and twelve from the NT, plus five questions on biblical interpretation and versions of the Bible. The survey was administered at the start of the semester. Almost 90 percent of the students came from homes in which at least one parent was a Christian.

The survey confirmed what the Bible professors at Northwest Nazarene College had suspected for a long time: "Bluntly stated, most of our young people are illiterate about the Bible" (Bowes 1997, 48). Here are four results from the survey that illustrate this point: 76 percent of the students could not name Israel's first king, 58 percent could not name one prophet for whom a book in the OT is named, 90 percent could not name the author of the book of Acts, and 41 percent could not name two of Jesus's disciples. The number of correct answers ranged from three to twenty-nine. All in all, 75 percent of the students answered sixteen or fewer questions correctly.

Since that original survey of college students, I have given the same questions to several adult Sunday school classes attended mostly by people who have been in church all their lives. The results were much better but still below what I had hoped for.

My article suggested several remedies for this problem as applied to children and youth, one of which had to do with preaching. The suggestion was this: more emphasis should be placed on the *teaching* component of every minister's preaching ministry. I enlarged on this thought with the following comments:

> Pastor, how do you view the teaching component of your pastoral ministry? Would a person who sat in your worship services for one year have a pretty good idea of what the Bible is about and what your theological position is on the great doctrines of the Church? Some pastors preach only from a few favorite books of the Bible. Other pastors jump around so much from topic to topic and book to book that people are left confused. They have no idea about the importance of David or Moses or Jeremiah or the times in which they lived or even who lived before the other one. It is true that some of this information is better learned during [the] Sunday School hour, but statistics tell us that many church people are not attending Sunday School. Maybe we need to reexamine the teaching aspect of our pulpit ministry. A series of five or six sermons several times a year on a biblical time period or a character like David or Moses or Jeremiah would help many laity to understand the progression of biblical history and the important individuals who participated in that history. (Bowes 1997, 49)

Now some twenty years after my article, Brent Strawn has written an excellent book that specifically focuses on biblical illiteracy of the OT among the adult population in the United States. He attributes this partially to a general lack of preaching from OT texts. The result is that "for many contemporary Christians, at least in North America, the Old Testament has ceased to function in healthy ways in their lives as sacred, authoritative, canonical literature" (Strawn 2017, 4-5). He goes on to say that "the Old

Testament is dying, if not already dead" (15). And further, "If the Old Testament dies, the New Testament will not be far behind it" (18).

Strawn's research is based on four pieces of evidence (19-58): (1) the US Religious Knowledge Survey produced by the Pew Forum on Religion and Public Life (2010), (2) a study of the Best Sermons series of books (1924-27, 1944-68, 1988-94), (3) an analysis of the treatment of the book of Psalms in contemporary musical worship, and (4) the usage of the OT in the *Revised Common Lectionary*.

Strawn makes five suggestions to help the church regain a proper understanding of the OT (2017, 213-42). They can be boiled down to two. First, the OT must be used far more frequently in preaching and teaching. Individual Christians will never accept the OT as a legitimate part of the canon if they only rarely encounter it in the church's ministry.

Second, the church must learn how to preach and teach the OT properly. Learning to understand the message of the OT does not happen automatically even with regular usage. There are many misinterpretations of the OT in modern Christendom. Too many interpretations leave the impression that the OT is inferior to the NT and thus not important. And too many sermons fail to take into account the characteristics of each major genre of OT literature—narratives, poetry, wisdom literature, prophecy, legal material, and short stories.

Each genre of Scripture requires a different methodology in sermon preparation. For example, a sermon from a narrative or a prophet should always place that passage in its historical context. And sermons from the poetic sections of the OT need to be aware of how parallelism, stanza divisions, and metaphorical language affect the meaning. In other words, *how* we preach and teach the OT is just as important as the frequency of usage. In addition, the OT must be preached and taught in a way that emphasizes the unity of the entire Bible and the importance of each individual book in contributing to the overall message.

If Strawn is correct, and I believe he is, the Christian church in North America needs to take some corrective action soon before it is too late. The death of the OT will have dire consequences. Every Christian preacher and teacher needs to consider carefully Strawn's call to action. Hopefully, this book on preaching from Job will contribute in some small way to a revival of more frequent usage and more proper usage of the OT in Christian pulpits today.

REFERENCES

Balentine, Samuel E. 2006. *Job*. Smyth and Helwys Bible Commentary. Macon, GA: Smyth and Helwys.
Blackwood, Andrew W., Jr. 1959. *Out of the Whirlwind: A Study of Job*. Grand Rapids: Baker Book House.
Bowes, A. Wendell. 1997. "What Are We Teaching Our Children about the Bible?" *The Preacher's Magazine* 73, no. 1 (September/October/November): 48-50.
———. 2018. *Job: A Commentary in the Wesleyan Tradition*. New Beacon Bible Commentary. Kansas City: Beacon Hill Press of Kansas City.
Calvin, John. 2011. *Sermons from Job*. Translated by Leroy Nixon. Pelham, AL: Solid Ground Christian Books.
Clines, David J. A. 1989. *Job 1-20*. Word Biblical Commentary, vol. 17. Dallas: Word Books.
———. 2006. *Job 21–37*. Word Biblical Commentary, vol. 18A. Nashville: Thomas Nelson.
———. 2011. *Job 38-42*. Word Biblical Commentary, vol. 18B. Nashville: Thomas Nelson.
Fee, Gordon D., and Douglas Stuart. 2014. *How to Read the Bible for All Its Worth: A Guide to Understanding the Bible*. 4th ed. Grand Rapids: Zondervan.
Goldingay, John. 2013. *Job for Everyone*. Old Testament for Everyone. Louisville, KY: Westminster John Knox.
Gordis, Robert. 1978. *The Book of Job: Commentary, New Translation, and Special Studies*. Moreshet Series: Studies in Jewish History, Literature and Thought 2. New York: Jewish Theological Seminary of America.
Hartley, John E. 1988. *The Book of Job*. New International Commentary on the Old Testament. Grand Rapids: Eerdmans.
Herion, Gary A. 1992. "Wrath of God." Pages 989-96 in vol. 6 of *The Anchor Bible Dictionary*, edited by David Noel Freedman. 6 vols. New York: Doubleday.
Holbert, John C. 1999. *Preaching Job*. St. Louis: Chalice.
Kidner, Derek. 1964. *The Proverbs: An Introduction and Commentary*. Tyndale Old Testament Commentaries. London: Tyndale.
McKeating, Henry. 1971. "The Central Issue of the Book of Job." *Expository Times* 82, no. 8 (May 1, 1971): 244-47.
McKenna, David L. 1986. *Job*. The Communicator's Commentary. Waco: Word Books.

References

Miller, Patrick D. 1994. *They Cried to the Lord: The Form and Theology of Biblical Prayer*. Minneapolis: Fortress.

Murphy, Roland E. 1977. *The Psalms, Job*. Proclamation Commentaries: The Old Testament Witnesses for Preaching. Philadelphia: Fortress.

Newsom, Carol A. 1996. "The Book of Job: Introduction, Commentary, and Reflections." Pages 317-637 in vol. 4 of *The New Interpreter's Bible*, edited by Leander E. Keck. 12 vols. Nashville: Abingdon.

Rad, Gerhard von. 1972. *Wisdom in Israel*. Translated by James D. Martin. Nashville: Abingdon.

Reyburn, William D. 1992. *A Handbook on the Book of Job*. New York: United Bible Societies.

Seow, C. L. 2013. *Job 1-21: Interpretation and Commentary*. Illuminations. Grand Rapids: Eerdmans.

Strawn, Brent A. 2017. *The Old Testament Is Dying: A Diagnosis and Recommended Treatment*. Grand Rapids: Baker Academic.

Ward, William B. 1958. *Out of the Whirlwind: A Study in the Book of Job*. Richmond, VA: John Knox.

Wesley, John. 1765. *Explanatory Notes upon the Old Testament*. Vol. 2. Bristol, UK: William Pine.

www.ingramcontent.com/pod-product-compliance
Lightning Source LLC
Chambersburg PA
CBHW070121100426
42744CB00010B/1887